50 *more* extreme brownies

recipes for the most over-the-top treats ever

connie weis

photography and design by alei rathjens

As will always be, this book, and any other
book I should write, is dedicated to my wonderful husband don,
who is the most amazing person I know.

Also, to jon and peter pruden,
who took over the ownership of the TASTE Family of Businesses
from my mentor, the late, great Peter Coe, and reimagined the business as
something bigger and better but still true to its soul.

my brownie . odyssey
continues...

Since my first book, *Extreme Brownies, 50 Recipes for the Most Over-the-Top Treats Ever* was published in 2014, one might think that my obsession for creating brownies and blondies was over.

In fact, it was just beginning.

Since then, I have been experimenting with so many exciting new ingredients and techniques that I felt compelled to write a second brownie cookbook.

New companies with different baking chocolates, cocoa powders, extracts, flavorings, and garnishes are popping up all the time, and I have experimented with as many as I could lay my hands on.

When I couldn't find an "add-in" for what I had in mind, I created my own: hence the different chocolate "barks" that found their way onto as well as into many of the brownies and blondies in this book. You'll find the barks are ridiculously easy to make, and you may want to use them as garnish for other treats, like cupcakes or ice cream. Full disclosure: sometimes I make them just for snacking...

I was alone when it came to baking as I was growing up, having lost my Mother at the age of 12. I pretty much made every mistake one could make: like trying to cream butter and sugar for cookies or cakes with butter straight from the refrigerator and hard as a rock, or leaving out key ingredients, like baking soda or baking powder, and wondering why my cakes came out of the oven at exactly the same height as when they went in.

To be fair, recipes were pretty sparse in instructions back then, and You Tube, much less computers, didn't eixst.

Therefore, I have tried to be as clear and explanatory as possible, in case you, young or novice baker, find yourself alone in your kitchen.

If there is one good thing that came out of the heartbreaking Coronavirus pandemic, it could be that families were able to spend more time together, and I hope some of that time was spent baking from scratch, and that possibly some of those bakes were brownies or blondies from my first book.

I have heard from at least two people that baked their way through all 50 recipes from *Extreme Brownies*.

Well, here are 50 extrem*er* recipes, so as they say on the Great British Bake Off: "ready, get set, BAKE!"

Very Best Wishes, and Happy Baking.

connie weis

the right
ingredients

Only with the best ingredients will you obtain the texture, richness, and depth of flavor of my Extreme Brownies. I have listed the exact brands of ingredients that I use and prefer, but in many cases, I offer an acceptable substitute that also worked very well. When a particular brand or percentage of chocolate is noted in a recipe, that is what worked best for me for that application. Different brands of cacao percentage chocolates melt and bake differently: a chocolate with a higher percentage of cacao will have a different viscosity than a lower percentage cacao chocolate. Trust me, and just go with the percentage cacao chocolate(s) as noted in each recipe.

As for add-ins, they of course can be substituted to your taste, but bear in mind that substitutions may alter the baking time by a few minutes one way or the other, so keep a close eye on your bake.

I am personally extravagant with garnishes, but they can be omitted or substituted at will.

baking chocolates

extra dark and bittersweet
I tested all of the recipes in this book using Guittard 63% Extra Dark Chocolate Baking Chips, and they are

my recommended chips when a bittersweet chocolate is called for. If using other brands, do not exceed 63% cacao mass. Acceptable substitute: Ghirardelli 60% Cacao Bittersweet Chocolate Chips.

unsweetened
There are few things in life I hate to do more than chop chocolate; so hats off to Guittard and Ghirardelli for finally providing home bakers with 100% Unsweetened Chocolate Chips, which are excellent and so convenient to use. Acceptable substitute: Ghirardelli or Baker's Unsweetened Baking Bars.

semi-sweet
Preferred: Guittard Semisweet Chocolate Chips. Acceptable substitute: Ghirardelli Semi-Sweet Chocolate Chips.

milk chocolate
Preferred: Guittard Milk Chocolate Baking Chips. Acceptable substitute: Ghirardelli Milk Chocolate Chips.

white chocolate
Full disclosure: I use Guittard Mystic White Chocolate Baking Wafers. They have delicious true "white chocolate" flavor and melt beautifully. They are available in 25# boxes through www.webstaurantstore. com. Alternately, I recommend Lindt CLASSIC RECIPE White Chocolate Bars, found in the candy aisle of most

grocery stores. Acceptable substitutes: Ghirardelli White Chocolate Premium Baking Bar or Ghirardelli CLASSIC WHITE Premium Baking Chips. Finely chopped white chocolate baking bars may not melt as smoothly as I prefer, but will still work very well in the recipes. Some recipes will call for specific "white or vanilla chips" for their melting or appearance qualities.

baking powder
Preferred: Rumford. Make sure that whatever baking powder you use has "aluminum free" on the label to avoid a tinny flavor.

cocoa powder
Preferred Dutch-processed: *Valrhona Pure Cocoa Powder. Acceptable substitute: Hershey's Special Dark Cocoa. Natural Unsweetened Cocoa Powder: Ghirardelli 100% Unsweetened Ground Cocoa. *Available through www.Amazon.com.

butter
Preferred: Land O Lakes or Challenge Unsweetened Butter. Avoid bargain/generic brands of butter; they often contain water which will strip your brownies of that coveted shiny sheen on top.

eggs
Large Cage-Free. It's the humane thing to do for the hens that provide our eggs. I buy mine at Costco.

flour
Preferred: King Arthur All Purpose Unbleached Flour. Acceptable substitutes: Pillsbury or Gold Medal Bleached Flour.

sugar
Preferred: Domino (C&H on the West coast) for all of my sugars. Acceptable substitute: Diixe Crystals. For granulated sugar, make sure the package indicates pure cane sugar.

salt
Use table salt, but never use iodized salt: it imparts a tinny flavor.

extracts and flavors
Cook's brand for all of my extracts and flavors. www.cooksvanilla.com.

crispearls
Preferred: Callebaut. Acceptable substitute: Baker's Choice Chocolate Balls. Available through: www.Amazon.com.

nuts

walnuts
Preferred: Diamond Shelled Walnuts. Acceptable substitute: Fisher Walnut Halves & Pieces.

peanuts
TASTE Signature Virginia Peanuts. www.tasteunlimited.com.

hazelnuts
Nature's Garden Roasted Hazelnuts Available through www.Amazon.com.

almonds
Blue Diamond Roasted Salted Almonds

the right
equipment

For the convenience of bakers everywhere, I have provided online purchasing sources. However, whenever possible, I buy from a local kitchen or department store, preferably independent, to help the stores stay in business and to maintain retail jobs for the people who work there, who are always at the ready to offer knowledgeable and personal assistance. I hope you will do the same and encourage your baking and cooking friends to do likewise.

baking pan

The same size pan is used for every item in this book, so buy a good quality heavy-weight aluminized steel pan. Do not bake brownies and blondies in a glass baking dish: the baking times and results will vary wildly. Recommended: Chicago Metallic Commercial II Traditional Uncoated Bake N' Roast Pan, 13 by 9 by 2-1/4-Inch. Available through www.Amazon.com.

bowls

mixing bowls

Melamine (hard plastic) mixing bowls that have a small spout for easy pouring. Recommended: Oggi Corporation 5286.1 White Melamine Mixing Bowl 3 Count Set. The smaller bowls will be used to weigh dry ingredients, and the large bowl is used to mix the batter. Available through www.Amazon.com

stainless steel bowl

2-quart (8½-inch round) stainless steel mixing bowl for creating the top for a double boiler. Recommended: American Metalcraft 2 qt Stainless Steel Mixing Bowl. Available through www.Amazon.com.

cutting board

Preferably white. Dishwasher safe nonporous polypropylene cutting board, that will be dedicated to only be used for cutting your brownies and blondies. Cutting boards that have been used for chopping garlic and onions will retain odor and taste no matter how well you wash them. Recommended: Farberware Poly Cutting Board, 12-Inch by 18-Inch, White. Available through www. Amazon.com.

mixers

hand mixer

Most of the frostings are made using a hand-held electric mixer. Any good quality hand-held mixer will do, but make sure the beaters are made from stainless steel or they can rust. Available in many department stores.

electric mixer

I have started making many of my blondies using a stand mixer since it adds volume and does a better job of incorporating the eggs, sugar, and melted butter than by doing it by hand with a whisk. Handmade marshmallow is made in a heavy-duty stand mixer using the paddle attachment, not the whisk attachment, which can break the tines apart as the marshmallow thickens. The paddle attachment will produce almost the same volume as the whisk attachment without the risk of breaking. Any good quality stand mixer will do, but I prefer the Kitchen-Aid 5-Qt. Available in many department stores.

knives

A 10-inch chef's knife used for cutting the slab, and a small 3 or 4-inch paring knife for running in between the foil and the pan to loosen and remove the slab. Recommended: J.A. Henckels International Classic 10-Inch Chef's Knife. Available through www.Amazon.com.

microwave-safe glass measuring cups

Both 1 and 2-cup sizes for melting chocolate in a microwave oven. Recommended: Pyrex Prepware 1 and 2-Cup Measuring Cups, Red Graphics, Clear. Available in many department stores.

measuring spoons

Two sets: one set for dry ingredients, and one set for wet. Take the spoons designated for dry ingredients off of the ring and leave the spoons designated for wet ingredients on the ring. Recommended: Cuisipro Stainless Steel Measuring Spoon Set. Available through www.Amazon.com.

saucepan

Heavy gauge (lightweight pans will burn the chocolate) stainless steel 2-quart saucepan for melting butter and chocolate together and to use as the bottom for a makeshift double boiler. Recommended: Cuisinart MultiClad Pro Stainless Steel 2-Quart Saucepan with Cover. Available through www.Amazon.com.

digital kitchen scale

You can use measuring cups and spoons for the recipes with good results, but using a scale makes for far more consistent and efficient baking. Recommended: Escali 157SS Arti Glass 15-Pound Capacity Digital Scale. Available through www.Amazon.com.

spatulas

silicone spatulas

One small and one large. Have specific colored silicone spatulas dedicated to baking purposes only. I use light-colored silicone spatulas for my baking tasks, and dark-colored silicone spatulas for pungent or savory ingredients. Buy spatulas with wood handles: I have had plastic-handled spatulas break on me at inopportune times. Available through www.Target.com.

small offset spatula

A must for smoothing brownie/blondie batter in the pan and spreading glazes, frostings, and handmade marshmallow. Recommended: Ateco 1385 Offset Spatula with 4.5-Inch Stainless Steel Blade, Wood Handle. Available through www.Amazon.com.

medium mesh strainer

It should fit inside and be able to rest in the small (1.5 liter) plastic mixing bowl, so it must be no wider than 6 inches across. Recommended: Norpro Stainless Steel 6-inch Strainer. Available through www.Amazon.com.

thermometers

candy thermometer

A must have for making handmade marshmallow. Recommended: Taylor 5983 Candy & Deep Fry Thermometer. Available through www.Amazon.com.

Decadent Dark Chocolate
Macadamia Nut Brownie

oven thermometer

An oven off by as little as 25 degrees results in a big difference in baking times and texture. Recommended: Taylor Precision Products Oven Dial Thermometer. Available through www.Amazon.com.

stainless steel whisks

Three sizes for three tasks: small whisk to blend melting chocolate and butter, medium whisk to blend the dry ingredients in the small mixing bowl, and large whisk to blend the batter in the large mixing bowl. Recommended: Norpro 2115 3-Piece Stainless Steel Balloon Wire Whisk Set. Available through www.Amazon.com.

nut chopper

Using a nut chopper is so convenient, especially when using a scale. Simple put the nut chopper on the scale, tare (subtract) off the weight of the chopper, and add your nuts to the chopper by weight. The nuts go through the grinding tines of the chopper only once, leaving the nut oils on the nuts and not on your cutting board. Recommended: Norpro Nut/Topping Chopper. Available through www.Amazon.com.

pastry comb

Not an essential tool, but a useful one. It can not only easily dress up your frostings, but by spreading the frosting back and forth with a pastry comb, it actually helps to level it out. Recommended: Ateco 1446 - 3 Sided Decorating Comb and 1447- 4 Sided Decorating Comb & Icing Smoother, 2 Pc Set. Available through www.Amazon.com.

pan preparation

Lining the pan with foil accomplishes two things: it makes it possible to remove the slab from the pan, and second, and possibly even more important, it is a sanitary way to bake your brownies and blondies. No matter how well the pan is cleaned, oily residue will build up and remain in the corner creases of the pan. Lining the pan with foil provides a perfectly clean interior for your baked goods each and every time the pan is used.

Materials needed to prepare a 9 by 13-inch pan include 12-inch wide heavy-duty aluminum foil and solid vegetable (not butter-flavored) shortening, like Crisco. Avoid pan sprays, as they tend to "pool" in places and have an unpleasant taste.

1   To prepare a 9 x 13 pan, turn the pan over on the counter; bottom side up. Tear off about a 16-inch length of aluminum foil. Position the foil (shiny side down) evenly over the bottom of the pan, and gently crease the foil over the edges, producing a foil template of the pan. For the corners, fold and neatly turn the foil in, much like "hospital corners" on a bed sheet. Set the prepared foil aside.

2   Using one finger, dab very small portions of Crisco on the interior bottom and sides of the pan. Then use your finger to spread the dabs around to entirely coat the interior with a very thin layer of shortening, which acts as a glue to hold the aluminum foil in place in the pan.

3   Press the foil onto the greased interior, smoothing out any wrinkles. The foil should extend about 1½ inches up each side of the pan. Very lightly grease the foil in the same manner used to prepare the pan for the foil.

techniques
(and cool tips)
for extreme baking perfection

1   Read the entire recipe prior to planning to bake. There's nothing more frustrating than starting a recipe and finding you don't have a necessary ingredient, utensil, or piece of equipment. Plus, you want to make sure that ingredients marked "room temperature" are indeed at room temperature and that you have allowed resting and chilling time for the slab as noted.

2   For best results, use a scale to weigh your ingredients. If you use measuring cups, spoon the flour into the measuring cup, then level off the top using a straight edge, such as the back of a steak knife or the side of a small offset spatula. Do not dip the measuring cup into the flour and level it off--that results in packing the flour, causing greater volume. Weights of cocoa powder vary greatly, but no matter what brand you choose, if you are measuring with a scale, use the weight as given in the recipe.

3   Have your eggs at room temperature. Cold eggs will do two undesirable things: they make the sugar (and salt) harder to dissolve, and they will quickly cool down the melted butter/chocolate mixture, causing a thicker batter that is hard to spread. The more you spread a brownie batter around in the pan (which is necessary to do as brownie batter is thicker than cake

batter and must be leveled out), the less likely you are to have that coveted shiny brownie top. I take the number of eggs needed for the recipe I'll be making out of the refrigerator the night before I plan to bake. I usually bake in the morning, so I want them ready to go when I am. Otherwise, it can take 2 to 3 hours for eggs to come to room temperature; especially if they're sitting on cold granite in a cool kitchen. To speed up the process, turn on the light (not the oven itself) in your oven and place the eggs on a kitchen towel on the middle rack. The oven will soon be much warmer than the kitchen and your eggs should be ready in an hour or less. A ready egg does not have sweat on it, and the egg should feel as if it's at room temperature when you hold it in the palm of your hand. I also take all other ingredients that will need to be at room temperature (like butter or cream cheese for a frosting), out of the refrigerator the night before I plan to bake.

4   Strain your granulated sugar. When weighing it out, place a medium-mesh strainer in the small mixing bowl, tare (subtract) off the weight of the bowl and strainer, and weigh the sugar through the strainer. After you strain out any large, coarse sugar granules, you may need to add more sugar. I save the coarse sugar granules in the strainer and transfer them to

an airtight container; to be used later in hot coffee, or as coarse sugar for the tops of muffins or coffee cakes. After the strained, granulated sugar is in the small mixing bowl, remove the strainer, and if the recipe calls for it, add the brown sugar to the bowl. Then use one impeccably clean hand to squeeze the brown sugar, looking for (and discarding) any large, hard lumps. Always add the salt to the center top of the weighed sugar(s). If you get distracted and can't remember if you added the salt, simply wet the tip of one finger and touch the center of the sugar. If it takes like salt, you know you added it.

5   After whisking in the melted butter/chocolate mixture into an egg mixture, take the whisk out of the bowl. Use a silicone spatula, not the whisk, to fold in the dry ingredients. And here's my "whisk trick": after the butter/chocolate mixture and vanilla have been whisked into the egg mixture, I rest the handle of the whisk on the granite backsplash of my counter with the tines of the whisk hanging over the spout of the large mixing bowl. Gravity is at work dropping the chocolate mixture on the whisk back into the bowl, while I am at work gathering the dry ingredients needed for the next step.

6   Different add-ins (or subtractions) will change the baking times. If you were more generous with chocolate chips or nuts than the recipe calls for, or you chose to leave out the "add-ins" altogether, your baking time will vary. Start checking the batter with a toothpick (I use round natural wood toothpicks for brownies and round colored wood toothpicks for blondies to better see the batters) 2 minutes before the designated recipe time and continue to check it every 2 minutes. Your slab is baked if the toothpick comes out clean or has a few crumbs on it when inserted in the center of the slab.

7   Always save the waxed wrapping that your butter sticks or pound butter bricks are packaged in-- keep them in the refrigerator. They make dandy disposable spoon rests for chocolate-covered whisks and spatulas and buttery knives. Disposable grease resistant 12x12-inch deli sandwich papers also work well for keeping your counter clean while baking.

Campfire S'more Brownies

how to
remove and cut the slab into extreme brownies or blondies

To get sharp, clean, cuts on brownies and blondies, the slab must be well chilled and taken out of the pan to be cut. Dragging a knife through the brownie or blondie slab while it is still in the pan cannot accomplish this desired presentation. For absolutely perfect edges, the knife should be cleaned in hot water and dried completely before each and every cut.

1   Before removing the slab from the pan, always chill your brownie/blondie slab very well (at least *7 to 8 hours) in advance. This makes the slab quite firm and easier to handle while removing it from the pan. Note: If you prefer your brownies to look more "cake-like" and not quite as dense, only chill them for about 3 hours before removing the slab from the pan and cutting.

2   To remove the brownie/blondie slab from the pan, run a thin knife between the foil and the sides of the pan, then turn the pan over on a sharp angle and push on the center of the pan, catching the top edge of the slab with your hand. Peel off and discard the foil and place the slab on a cutting board.

3   I cut off (and eat) about ¼ to ½-inch of the sides that contained the corners of the baked slab, which tend to be a bit dryer. I use a clear 18-inch long ruler (Helix Acrylic 18 inch/45cm Office Ruler) to find the center of the remaining slab, then use a small, sharp knife to lightly score the slab on each side to mark where to make my first cut. Using the small knife marks as a guide, place a 10-inch chef's knife directly over the middle of the slab and press the knife evenly down through the slab. You now have two equal-sized halves.

4   Cut each half in half in the same manner, then cut the four long quarters into three equal pieces. You now have twelve (approixmately) 2¾-inch-square generous brownies or blondies. For bite-size squares, cut each well-chilled brownie or blondie into quarters.

how to
store, freeze, ship, and gift extreme brownies or blondies

As for a great cheese, the taste and texture of brownies and blondies are best appreciated at room temperature. Store them chilled or frozen, but let them come to room temperature before serving.

storing

Store your cut brownies and blondies in the refrigerator in an airtight food storage container with wax paper between each layer. Those with a delicate frosting, cheesecake, or sticky top, should be placed individually on *patty papers and stored, without stacking, in airtight containers. Note: Patty papers are individually cut sheets of waxed paper that are widely used in restaurants to separate and store hamburger patties. I use Handy Wacks 5x4¾-inch patty papers, which come in a box of 1,000 sheets. Available at most restaurant supply stores and www.Amazon.com.

freezing

Every item in this book (including those with cheesecake layers or handmade marshmallow) may be frozen without compromising the flavor or texture if done properly. For those items with a firm top surface or chocolate glaze, I freeze them in packages of six: I place six well-chilled brownies (two side-by-side strips of three) on an *18-inch wide large sheet of plastic wrap. Bring the wrap tightly up over the brownies to completely cover and tuck in the sides. Place the wrapped 6-pack in a freezer-safe plastic bag and seal tightly. Use a Sharpie to label and date the contents on your freezer bag. Note: I use Reynolds 914 PVC 2,000 feet long by 18-inch wide Clear Wrap. Available at most restaurant supply stores and www.Amazon.com.

For frosted, fragile, or sticky-topped items, place each brownie or blondie on a patty paper, then place them in a container that allows them to be stored without the top surface of the item touching the lid, such as a plastic food storage container or pristine *pizza box. If using a pizza box, after filling it with your brownies or blondies, place the box on a large sheet of plastic wrap and completely wrap the pizza box or container. Use freezer tape and a Sharpie to label and date the contents of your wrapped plastic container or pizza box. Freeze for up to three months. Thaw at room temperature (unwrapped) for 1 hour, or thaw (wrapped) in the refrigerator overnight. Note: I use 10 by 10-inch corrugated cardboard pizza boxes packed 50 boxes to a bundle. Available at most restaurant supply stores and www.Amazon.com.

shipping

This whole brownie gig started many years ago when I started shipping tins of brownies to friends and family members at Christmas. I try to ship only in colder weather, but if you are shipping in warmer climates, shipping stores are prepared with Styrofoam-lined boxes and freezer packs. I only ship brownies that I can wrap tightly in plastic wrap, which includes any with a firm top surface or chocolate glaze. Never ship items with a shorter shelf life; for example, those that contain more perishable elements, such as fresh fruit sauces or cheesecake layers. Place the wrapped brownies or blondies in a decorative tin (or box) and completely wrap the outside of the tin in plastic wrap. Place the wrapped tin in the center of a sturdy box surrounded with bubble wrap or inflated plastic air pillows for protection while shipping. The wrapped brownies are fine at room temperature for 5 to 7 days, so find out how long it will take your package to arrive at its destination. Tell the recipient to place their brownies and blondies in the refrigerator when they receive their package to extend the shelf life of the baked goods. If an enclosure card is included, write the names of the items in your tin, and if you really want to score big, include a copy of my book (or books) with sticky notes on the pages of the baked items you are gifting. I always ship my brownies and blondies on a Monday to make sure that they are not languishing in a hot warehouse over the weekend. My friend at the shipping store told me that the box will be handled with more care if marked FRAGILE rather than PERISHABLE, so that's what I write on the outside of the box.

gifting

For the best gift presentation of an individual brownie or blondie, choose one with a firm top surface or chocolate glaze, tear off about a 10-inch length of 12-inch wide plastic wrap and place it on a flat surface. Place the brownie or blondie, top surface down, on the plastic and tightly wrap the item, with the excess wrap on the back/bottom of the brownie or blondie. Many craft stores (like Michael's) have a great selection of individual bags, boxes, and ribbons to turn an individual brownie or blondie into a "sweet" little gift.

If I am going to a party, it's a given that I will be bringing brownies and blondies. I cut them into bite-size pieces and attractively arrange them on an inexpensive plastic tray that need not be returned. Dollar stores have a nice assortment.

Finally, for a Bridal shower or birthday, I can be counted on to gift a 9 by 13-inch baking pan with a couple of spatulas (both silicone and small metal offset) and copies of my books nestled inside.

contents

brownies

blondies

brownies

connie's improved caramel-stuffed sea salt brownies

makes 12 large squares or 24 smaller bars

It always bothered me that my number one best-seller was the shortest brownie I sold. I increased the amount of batter so that it now cozies up to the same level as my other brownies. Who says you can't improve on perfection?

---

caramel layer
2 tablespoons (1 ounce) unsalted butter
3 tablespoons (1.5 ounces) heavy whipping cream
13 ounces (about 45) caramel candies (Kraft Traditional Caramels)
½ teaspoon pure vanilla extract

brownie batter
Vegetable shortening for pan
2½ sticks (10 ounces) unsalted butter
¾ cup (4 ounces) 100% cacao unsweetened chocolate chips
1¼ cups (7.5 ounces) 63% extra dark chocolate chips
5 large eggs, at room temperature
1¼ cups (8.7 ounces) granulated sugar
1¼ packed cups (10 ounces) light brown sugar
1 teaspoon salt
2 teaspoons pure vanilla extract
1¼ cups (5.6 ounces) unbleached all-purpose flour
½ teaspoon and 1/8 teaspoon baking powder

milk chocolate glaze
5 teaspoons (0.07 ounce) canola oil
1½ cups (9 ounces) milk chocolate chips

garnish
1½ teaspoons sea salt flakes (Maldon)

1   To make the caramel layer, cut the butter into ¼-inch slices. Place the butter slices and cream in a 2-quart saucier or saucepan. Begin to melt the mixture over very low heat. Unwrap the caramels, and as each is unwrapped, add it to the mixture. Cook over medium-low heat, stirring occasionally with a silicone spatula. While the caramels are slowly melting, proceed with the brownie batter. Finish preparing the caramel once the brownie base is in the oven.

2   Adjust an oven rack to the middle level of the oven and preheat to 350°F. Prepare a 9 by 13-inch baking pan with heavy-duty aluminum foil as shown on page ix. Lightly grease the foil in the pan.

3   To make the brownie batter, cut the butter sticks into ½-inch slices. In a small, heavy saucepan, begin to melt the butter pieces over the lowest setting; add the unsweetened and extra dark chocolate chips. Stir with a small whisk until combined and the chocolate is melted and smooth. Turn off the heat, but leave the saucepan on the burner while proceeding with the recipe.

4   Using a large whisk, lightly beat the eggs in a large mixing bowl. Place the sugars and salt in a separate small mixing bowl, then whisk into the eggs just until incorporated. Briefly whisk the melted chocolate mixture, then gradually whisk into the egg mixture until just combined. Briefly whisk in the vanilla.

5   Place the flour and baking powder in the small mixing bowl; whisk together to combine. Sift through a medium strainer directly onto the batter; stir in with a silicone spatula until just combined. Pour half (1 pound 10 ounces) of the brownie batter into the prepared pan. The best way to do this is by weight. Place the prepared pan on a scale, tare off (subtract) the weight of the pan, and scrape the correct weight of batter directly into the pan. Spread the batter evenly with a small offset spatula. Bake for 16 minutes, until a toothpick inserted in the center of the slab comes out clean. Finish the caramel layer while the brownie base is baking.

6   To finish the caramel layer, once the caramels are melted and completely smooth, stir in the vanilla. Set the pan with the caramel aside.

7   After the bottom brownie layer has baked for 16 minutes, transfer the pan to a cooling rack. Pour the cooked caramel over the hot brownie base and spread evenly with a small offset spatula. Dollop the remaining brownie batter evenly over the caramel layer and carefully spread to the edges with the offset spatula, covering the caramel layer. Return the pan to the oven and bake an additional 25 minutes, until a toothpick inserted in the center comes out clean. Transfer the pan to a cooling rack.

8   To make the milk chocolate glaze, bring a medium saucepan with two inches of water just to a boil. Place the canola oil and milk chocolate chips in a metal mixing bowl that will fit over the saucepan to form a double boiler. When the water comes to a boil, take the saucepan off the heat and place the mixing bowl over the hot water: the bottom of the metal bowl should not touch the hot water. Stir with a small silicone spatula until the chocolate is melted and perfectly smooth. Remove the mixing bowl from the saucepan and using a kitchen towel, wipe off any condensation from the bottom of the mixing bowl. Pour the glaze over the top of the warm brownie slab and spread evenly with a small offset spatula, then sprinkle the sea salt over the glaze. Refrigerate the pan for 7 to 8 hours, or overnight. See page xii for instructions on removing and cutting the slab, and for refrigerated storage (up to 2 weeks) and freezing guidelines. Note: The caramel next to the pan's sides gets hard and is unpleasant to eat; cut off and discard all of the edges around the brownie slab.

Connie's Improved Caramel-Stuffed
Sea Salt Brownies

coconut macaroon brownies

makes 12 large squares or 24 smaller bars

Yes, I divulged my top secret recipe for my best-selling Caramel-Stuffed Sea Salt Brownies in my first book, Extreme Brownies: 50 Recipes for the Most Over-the-Top Treats Ever, but I just couldn't bring myself to divulge the recipe for my own personal favorite, Coconut Macaroon Brownies. My loyal customers immediately noticed the ahem, oversight, and protested. This brownie came about when I took my chewy yet crunchy coconut macaroon batter and plopped it on top of a brownie, creating a hybrid treat that rocks my world. Now it can (finally) rock yours.

coconut for the macaroon layer
1 (14-ounce) bag sweetened coconut flakes

brownie batter
Vegetable shortening for pan
2½ sticks (10 ounces) unsalted butter
1²/₃ cups (10 ounces) 63% extra dark chocolate chips
5 large eggs, at room temperature
2½ cups (1 pound 1.5 ounces) sugar
1 teaspoon salt
2 teaspoons pure vanilla extract
1 cup (4 ounces) cake flour
1 cup (4 ounces Dutch-processed unsweetened cocoa powder

coconut macaroon batter
1 cup (10 ounces) sweetened condensed milk
¼ teaspoon salt
2 teaspoons pure vanilla extract
¼ teaspoon pure almond extract
2 large egg whites, at room temperature
2 tablespoons sugar

bittersweet chocolate glaze
3½ teaspoons (0.05 ounce) canola oil
1 cup (6 ounces) 60% cacao bittersweet chocolate chips

1 To toast the coconut, adjust an oven rack to the middle level of the oven and preheat to 350°F. Spread the coconut out evenly onto a half-sheet pan. Bake for 5 minutes, then turn the coconut with a thin metal spatula, bringing the coconut from the outer edges of the pan into the center. Bake for 5

additional minutes; repeat turning the coconut, then continue to bake in 2 minute intervals, turning the coconut, until the coconut is uniformly golden brown and quite a bit of the coconut is toasted brown and crunchy. Transfer the pan to a cooling rack and let cool at room temperature. Maintain the oven temperature at 350°F.

2   Cut out a sheet of parchment paper to measure 9½ x 13½ inches. Lightly grease the bottom and interior sides of a 9 by 13-inch baking pan with a *removable bottom. Place the parchment paper on the bottom of the pan to come ¼-inch up the sides of the pan. Lightly grease the parchment paper. Set aside. Note: If you don't have a pan with a removable bottom, prepare a regular 9 by 13-inch pan with foil as directed on page ix. The problem with this is the coconut macaroon layer will shrink as it bakes and pull the foil in with it slightly, but this will still work for the recipe. Using a pan prepared as above keeps the coconut macaroon layer evenly against the sides of the pan.

3   To make the brownie batter, cut the butter sticks into ½-inch slices. In a small, heavy saucepan, begin to melt the butter pieces over the lowest setting; add the extra dark chocolate chips. Stir with a small whisk until combined and the chocolate is melted and smooth. Turn off the heat, but leave the saucepan on the burner while proceeding with the recipe.

4   Using a large whisk, lightly beat the eggs in a large mixing bowl. Place the sugar and salt in a separate small mixing bowl, then whisk into the eggs just until incorporated. Briefly whisk the melted chocolate mixture, then gradually whisk into the egg mixture until just combined. Briefly whisk in the vanilla.

5   Place the flour and cocoa powder in the small mixing bowl; whisk together to combine. Sift through a medium strainer directly onto the batter; stir in with a

silicone spatula until just combined. Pour the batter into the prepared pan and spread evenly with a small offset spatula. Bake for 34 minutes, until a toothpick inserted in the center of the slab comes out clean. Transfer the pan to a cooling rack. Maintain the oven temperature at 350°F.

6   To make the coconut macaroon batter, place the condensed milk, salt, vanilla, and almond extract in a large mixing bowl; stir well with a silicone spatula to combine. Set aside ¼ cup (0.05 ounce) of the toasted coconut to use later for garnish. Add the remaining toasted coconut to the condensed milk mixture and stir well to combine.

7   Using a stand mixer fitted with the whisk attachment, beat the egg whites on medium speed just until they are foamy. Increase the speed to medium-high and add the sugar, one tablespoon at a time. Increase the speed to high and beat until the whites are stiff and glossy, but not dry. Dollop the egg whites onto the coconut mixture; fold in well.

8   Dollop the coconut macaroon batter over the warm slab, then use a small offset spatula to spread the coconut macaroon batter evenly to completely cover the slab. Return the pan to the oven and bake an additional 18 minutes, until the top is lightly browned and the coconut macaroon mixture is firm and lightly cracked around the edges. Transfer the pan to a cooling rack.

9   To make the bittersweet chocolate glaze, bring a medium saucepan with two inches of water just to a boil. Place the canola oil and chocolate chips in a metal mixing bowl that will fit over the saucepan to form a double boiler. When the water comes to a boil, take the saucepan off the heat and place the mixing bowl over the hot water: the bottom of the metal bowl should not touch the hot water. Stir with a small silicone spatula until the chocolate is melted

and perfectly smooth. Remove the mixing bowl from the saucepan and using a kitchen towel, wipe off any condensation from the bottom of the mixing bowl. Pour the glaze over the top of the coconut macaroon layer. Use a small offset spatula to spread the glaze evenly, then sprinkle the reserved toasted coconut evenly over the glaze. Refrigerate the pan for 7 to 8 hours, or overnight.

10 To remove the brownie slab from the pan, run a thin knife between the slab and the sides of the pan. Push the bottom of the pan up out of the sides and place it on a cutting board. Use a long chef's knife to cut it into 12 large squares, cleaning the knife in hot water and drying before each cut to provide sharp clean edges. See page xiv for refrigerated storage (up to 2 weeks) and freezing guidelines.

Coconut Macaroon
Brownies

nutella-stuffed brownies

makes 12 large squares or 24 smaller bars

My Caramel-Stuffed Sea Salt Brownies were such a hit I soon started thinking about what other goodies I could stuff in a brownie. I have yet to meet a person who doesn't like Nutella, so it was an obvious choice. If you don't want to make the chocolate hazelnut bark, substitute two (any size) chocolate hazelnut candy bars.

chocolate hazelnut bark
Vegetable shortening for pan
$2/3$ cup (3 ounces) skinned and roasted whole hazelnuts (Nature's Garden)
1 tablespoon (0.04 ounce) canola oil
¾ cup and 2 tablespoons (5 ounces) milk chocolate chips
½ teaspoon sea salt flakes (Maldon)

brownie batter
Vegetable shortening for pan
2½ sticks (10 ounces) unsalted butter
¾ cup (4 ounces) 100% cacao unsweetened chocolate chips
1¼ cups (7.5 ounces) 63% extra dark chocolate chips
5 large eggs, at room temperature
1¼ cups (8.7 ounces) granulated sugar
1¼ packed cups (10 ounces) light brown sugar
1 teaspoon salt
1 teaspoon pure vanilla extract
1 teaspoon hazelnut flavor
1¼ cups (5.6 ounces) unbleached all-purpose flour
½ teaspoon and $1/8$ teaspoon baking powder
1½ cups (16.5 ounces) chocolate hazelnut spread (Nutella)

milk chocolate glaze
5 teaspoons (0.07 ounce) canola oil
1½ cups (9 ounces) milk chocolate chips

1   To make the chocolate hazelnut bark, cut out a sheet of parchment paper to line the bottom of a quarter sheet pan. Lightly grease the bottom of the pan and place the parchment paper on top; press down to secure the paper onto the pan. Set aside.

2   Using a nut chopper or chef's knife, finely chop the hazelnuts. Set aside.

3   Bring a medium saucepan with two inches of water just to a boil. Place the canola oil and milk chocolate chips in a metal mixing bowl that will fit over the saucepan to form a double boiler. When the water comes to a boil, take the saucepan off the heat and place the mixing bowl over the hot water: the bottom of the metal bowl should not touch the hot water. Stir with a small silicone spatula until the milk chocolate is melted and perfectly smooth. Stir in the chopped hazelnuts. Remove the mixing bowl from

the saucepan and using a kitchen towel, wipe off any condensation from the bottom of the mixing bowl. Scrape the mixture onto the parchment-lined pan. Using a small offset spatula, spread the chocolate evenly to about 1/8-inch thickness. Sprinkle the sea salt evenly over the warm chocolate. Refrigerate the pan while proceeding with the recipe. Note: Set aside the saucepan, metal mixing bowl, and small spatula (no need to wash them) to use later for the milk chocolate glaze.

4   Adjust an oven rack to the middle level of the oven and preheat to 350°F. Prepare a 9 by 13-inch baking pan with heavy-duty aluminum foil as shown on page ix. Lightly grease the foil in the pan.

5   To make the brownie batter, cut the butter sticks into ½-inch slices. In a small, heavy saucepan, begin to melt the butter pieces over the lowest setting; add the unsweetened and extra dark chocolate chips. Stir with a small whisk until combined and the chocolate is melted and smooth. Turn off the heat, but leave the saucepan on the burner while proceeding with the recipe.

6   Using a large whisk, lightly beat the eggs in a large mixing bowl. Place the sugars and salt in a separate small mixing bowl, then whisk into the eggs just until incorporated. Briefly whisk the melted chocolate mixture, then gradually whisk into the egg mixture until just combined. Briefly whisk in the vanilla and hazelnut flavor.

7   Place the flour and baking powder in the small mixing bowl; whisk together to combine. Sift through a medium strainer directly onto the batter; stir in with a silicone spatula until just combined. Pour half (1 pound 10 ounces) of the brownie batter into the prepared pan. The best way to do this is by weight. Place the prepared pan on a scale, tare off (subtract) the weight of the pan, and scrape the correct

weight of batter directly into the pan. Spread the batter evenly with a small offset spatula. Bake for 16 minutes, until a toothpick inserted in the center of the slab comes out clean.

8   After the bottom brownie layer has baked for 16 minutes, transfer the pan to a cooling rack. Dollop the Nutella over the hot brownie base and spread evenly with a small offset spatula. Dollop the remaining brownie batter evenly over the Nutella and carefully spread to the edges with the offset spatula, covering the Nutella. Return the pan to the oven and bake an additional 25 minutes, until a toothpick inserted in the center of the slab comes out clean. Transfer the pan to a cooling rack.

9   To make the milk chocolate glaze, bring the medium saucepan with two inches of water just to a boil. Place the canola oil and milk chocolate chips in the reserved metal mixing bowl. When the water comes to a boil, take the saucepan off the heat and place the mixing bowl over the hot water; the bottom of the metal bowl should not touch the hot water. Stir with a small silicone spatula until the milk chocolate is melted and perfectly smooth. Remove the mixing bowl from the saucepan and using a kitchen towel, wipe off any condensation from the bottom of the mixing bowl. Pour the glaze over the top of the warm brownie slab. Using a small offset spatula, spread the glaze evenly. Place the pan in the refrigerator for 20 minutes to cool down the glaze. Note: Chop the chocolate hazelnut bark while the glaze is cooling.

10 Using the parchment paper, transfer the chilled bark to a cutting board. Using a large chef's knife, coarsely chop the bark into approximate ¼-inch dice. Place the chopped bark in a small bowl and place in the freezer to chill while the glaze continues to cool in the refrigerator.

Nutella-Stuffed
Brownies

11 Sprinkle the chopped bark evenly over the glaze.
Refrigerate the pan for 7 to 8 hours, or overnight. See
page xii for instructions on removing and cutting the
slab, and for refrigerated storage (up to 2 weeks) and
freezing guidelines.

road trip pretzel brownies

makes 12 large squares or 24 smaller bars

When I go on long trips, if possible, I would always rather drive than fly, and when I do, I leave nothing to chance. On the back seat I have a cooler stocked with my favorite drinks and cheeses as well as a bag with my favorite potato chips and crackers. Not surprisingly, I always include something sweet, so these beauties are usually packed in the cooler. They're a cross between a brownie and a candy bar, so what could be better?

brownie batter
Vegetable shortening for pan
2½ sticks (10 ounces) unsalted butter
¾ cup (4 ounces) 100% cacao unsweetened chocolate chips
1¼ cups (7.5 ounces) 63% extra dark chocolate chips
5 large eggs, at room temperature
1¼ cups (8.7 ounces) granulated sugar
1¼ packed cups (10 ounces) light brown sugar
1 teaspoon salt
2 teaspoons pure vanilla extract
1¼ cups (5.6 ounces) unbleached all-purpose flour
½ teaspoon and 1/8 teaspoon baking powder
40 (8.5 ounces) dark chocolate covered mini pretzels (Liberty Bell or Trader Joe's)

caramel layer
2 tablespoons (1 ounce) unsalted butter
3 tablespoons (1.5 ounces) heavy whipping cream
13 ounces (about 45) caramel candies (Kraft Traditional Caramels)
½ teaspoon pure vanilla extract

pretzel sticks
(never "butter" flavored)

roasted salted virginia peanuts

bittersweet chocolate drizzle
2 teaspoons (0.03 ounce) canola oil
½ cup (3 ounces) 60% cacao bittersweet chocolate chips

garnish
Morton Coarse Sea Salt

1   Adjust an oven rack to the middle level of the oven and preheat to 350°F. Prepare a 9 by 13-inch baking pan with heavy-duty aluminum foil as shown on page ix. Lightly grease the foil in the pan.

2   To make the brownie batter, cut the butter sticks into ½-inch slices. In a small, heavy saucepan, begin to melt the butter pieces over the lowest setting; add the unsweetened and extra dark chocolate chips. Stir with a small whisk until combined and the chocolate

Road Trip
Pretzel Brownies

is melted and smooth. Turn off the heat, but leave the saucepan on the burner while proceeding with the recipe.

3   Using a large whisk, lightly beat the eggs in a large mixing bowl. Place the sugars and salt in a separate small mixing bowl, then whisk into the eggs just until incorporated. Briefly whisk the melted chocolate mixture, then gradually whisk into the egg mixture until just combined. Briefly whisk in the vanilla.

4   Place the flour and baking powder in the small mixing bowl; whisk together to combine. Sift through a medium strainer directly onto the batter; stir in with a silicone spatula until just combined. Pour half (1 pound 10 ounces) of the brownie batter into the prepared pan. The best way to do this is by weight. Place the prepared pan on a scale, tare off (subtract) the weight of the pan, and scrape the correct weight of batter directly into the pan.

5   Place the chocolate covered pretzels over the batter in eight rows of five pretzels each: do not place any within ½-inch of the pan sides. Dollop the remaining brownie batter evenly over the pretzels and carefully spread to the edges with the offset spatula, covering the pretzels. Bake for 34 minutes, until a toothpick inserted in the center of the slab comes out clean. Transfer the pan to a cooling rack. Note: Make the caramel layer while the brownie slab is baking.

6   To make the caramel layer, cut the butter into ¼-inch slices. Place the butter slices and cream in a 2-quart saucier or saucepan. Begin to melt the mixture over very low heat. Unwrap the caramels, and as each is unwrapped, add it to the mixture. Cook over medium-low heat, stirring occasionally with a silicone spatula, until the caramels are melted and completely smooth. Stir in the vanilla.

7   Pour the cooked caramel over the hot brownie base and spread evenly with a small offset spatula. Immediately position the pretzel sticks in random groups of 3 side-by-side across the caramel. Place some whole peanuts randomly in between the pretzel groups.

8   To make the bittersweet chocolate drizzle, pour the oil into a 1-cup Pyrex measuring cup; add the bittersweet chocolate chips. Microwave on 50% power for 3 minutes, then stir with a small whisk or silicone spatula until the chips are melted and completely smooth. Pour the chocolate through a small plastic funnel into a small (6-ounce) plastic squeeze bottle. Using the plastic bottle, squeeze the chocolate over the pretzels in a back and forth motion. Sparingly sprinkle coarse sea salt over the chocolate drizzle. Refrigerate the pan for 7 to 8 hours, or overnight. See page xiv for refrigerated storage (up to 2 weeks) and freezing guidelines.

note

Instead of using a plastic bottle, the spatula can be used to randomly drizzle the melted chocolate over the pretzels.

cosmos brownies

makes 12 large squares or 24 smaller bars

This is my take on those packaged "Cosmic" Brownies that you find in most grocery stores, usually at the end of an aisle. Since I have made brownies for a living, I never bought a package until recently because I wanted to create my own version. Sadly, they were not to my liking. However! There are many times that Debbie and I are very good friends; just not when it comes to brownies.

brownie batter

Vegetable shortening for pan
3 sticks (12 ounces) unsalted butter
¾ cup and 1 tablespoon (5 ounces) 100% cacao unsweetened chocolate chips
1½ cups (9 ounces) 63% extra dark chocolate chips
6 large eggs, at room temperature
1½ cups (10.5 ounces) granulated sugar
1½ packed cups (12 ounces) light brown sugar
1¼ teaspoons salt
1 tablespoon pure vanilla extract
1½ cups (6.8 ounces) unbleached all-purpose flour
¾ teaspoon baking powder

chocolate glaze

6 tablespoons (3 ounces) unsalted butter
1 tablespoon (0.08 ounce) light corn syrup
1 cup (6 ounces) 60% cacao bittersweet chocolate chips

garnish

3 tablespoons rainbow candy coated chips
*If unavailable, substitute one (1.77-ounce) tube of mini M&M's

1   Adjust an oven rack to the middle level of the oven and preheat to 350°F. Prepare a 9 by 13-inch baking pan with heavy-duty aluminum foil as shown on page ix. Lightly grease the foil in the pan.

2   To make the brownie batter, cut the butter sticks into ½-inch slices. In a small, heavy saucepan, melt the butter pieces over the lowest setting; add the unsweetened and extra dark chocolate chips. Stir with a small whisk until combined and the chocolate is melted and smooth. Turn off the heat, but leave the saucepan on the burner while proceeding with the recipe.

3   Using a large whisk, lightly beat the eggs in a large mixing bowl. Place the sugars and salt in a separate small mixing bowl, then whisk into the eggs just until incorporated. Briefly whisk the melted chocolate mixture, then gradually whisk into the egg mixture until just combined. Briefly whisk in the vanilla. Note: Set aside the saucepan and small whisk (no need to wash them) to use later for the chocolate glaze.

Cosmos Brownies

4   Place the flour and baking powder in the small mixing bowl; whisk together to combine. Sift through a medium strainer directly onto the batter; stir in with a silicone spatula until just combined. Pour the batter into the prepared pan and spread evenly with a small offset spatula. Bake for 37 minutes, until a toothpick inserted in the center of the slab comes out clean. Transfer the pan to a cooling rack.

5   To make the chocolate glaze, slice the butter into ¼-inch slices. Place the butter slices and corn syrup in the reserved small saucepan and melt over the lowest setting. Meanwhile, place the chocolate chips in a 2-cup Pyrex measuring cup. Microwave the chips on high power for 90 seconds, whisk with the reserved small whisk, then microwave an additional 15 seconds: whisk again. Pour the melted butter mixture into the melted chocolate and whisk gently until combined and completely smooth. Pour the glaze over the warm brownie slab and spread evenly with a small offset spatula. Let the glazed slab sit at room temperature for 10 minutes to cool down slightly, then distribute the candy coated chips evenly over the glaze. Refrigerate the pan for 7 to 8 hours, or overnight. See page xii for instructions on removing and cutting the slab, and for refrigerated storage (up to 2 weeks) and freezing guidelines.

mad about milk chocolate brownies

makes 12 large squares or 24 smaller bars

I am mad about milk chocolate. I discovered this very early on in my childhood when one year I couldn't stop eating one of the tall milk chocolate bunnies in my Easter basket. I started nibbling on his ears (where else?) and gnawed my way all the way down to his rabbit feet. As I've grown older, I have become more particular about the milk chocolate I consume and veer towards higher end artisanal bars, but having toured the Hershey chocolate factory several times as a child, a good old Hershey's candy bar still hits the spot more often than I care to admit.

---

crispy milk chocolate bark
Vegetable shortening for pan
1 tablespoon (0.04 ounce) canola oil
1 cup (6 ounces) milk chocolate chips
1 cup (0.09 ounce) sweetened toasted rice cereal
    (Frosted Krispies)

brownie batter
Vegetable shortening for pan
2¼ sticks (10 ounces) unsalted butter
3$^1/_3$ cups (1 pound 4 ounces) milk chocolate chips
5 large eggs, at room temperature
½ cup and 2 tablespoons (4.4 ounces) granulated sugar
1¼ packed cups (10 ounces) light brown sugar
1 teaspoon salt
1 teaspoon pure vanilla extract
1 teaspoon pure chocolate extract
2 cups (9 ounces) unbleached all-purpose flour
1 teaspoon baking powder
3 tablespoons Dutch-processed unsweetened
    cocoa powder

milk chocolate ganache
1$^2/_3$ cups (10 ounces) milk chocolate chips
½ cup (4 ounces) heavy whipping cream

1   To make the crispy milk chocolate bark, cut out a sheet of parchment paper to line the bottom of a quarter sheet pan. Lightly grease the bottom of the pan and place the parchment paper on top; press down to secure the paper onto the pan. Set aside.

2   Bring a medium saucepan with two inches of water just to a boil. Place the canola oil and milk chocolate chips in a metal mixing bowl that will fit over the saucepan to form a double boiler. When the water comes to a boil, take the saucepan off the heat and place the mixing bowl over the hot water: the bottom of the metal bowl should not touch the hot water. Stir with a small silicone spatula until the chocolate is

melted and perfectly smooth. Stir in the rice cereal. Remove the mixing bowl from the saucepan and using a kitchen towel, wipe off any condensation from the bottom of the mixing bowl. Scrape the mixture onto the parchment-lined pan. Using a small offset spatula, spread the chocolate evenly to about ¼-inch thickness. Refrigerate the pan while proceeding with the recipe.

3   Adjust an oven rack to the middle level of the oven and preheat to 350°F. Prepare a 9 by 13-inch baking pan with heavy-duty aluminum foil as shown on page ix. Lightly grease the foil in the pan.

4   To make the brownie batter, cut the butter sticks into ½-inch slices. In a small, heavy saucepan melt the butter pieces over the lowest setting. Add the milk chocolate chips to the melted butter, stirring constantly with a small whisk until melted. When the milk chocolate is melted and completely smooth, turn off the heat, but leave the saucepan on the burner while proceeding with the recipe.

5   Using a large whisk, lightly beat the eggs in a large mixing bowl. Place the sugars and salt in a separate small mixing bowl, then whisk into the eggs just until incorporated. Briefly whisk the melted chocolate mixture, then gradually whisk into the egg mixture until just combined. Briefly whisk in the extracts. Note: Set aside the saucepan (no need to wash it) to use later for the milk chocolate ganache.

6   Place the flour, baking powder, and cocoa powder in the small mixing bowl; whisk together to combine. Sift through a medium strainer directly onto the batter; stir in with a silicone spatula until just combined. Pour the batter into the prepared pan and spread evenly with a small offset spatula. Bake for 42 minutes, until a toothpick inserted in the center of the slab comes out clean. Transfer the pan to a cooling rack.

7   To make the milk chocolate ganache, place the milk chocolate chips in a small bowl. Set aside.

8   Place the cream in the reserved saucepan. Bring the cream just to a simmer; do not let it boil. Take the pan off of the heat and add the milk chocolate chips. Shake the pan slightly to cover the chips with the cream. Cover the pan with a lid and let sit for 2 minutes. Return the pan to the burner (with the heat turned off) and blend together with a small silicone spatula just until the chips are incorporated and completely melted. Pour the ganache over the warm brownie slab and spread evenly with a small offset spatula. Place the pan in the refrigerator for 20 minutes to cool down the ganache. Note: Chop the crispy milk chocolate bark while the ganache is cooling.

9   Using the parchment paper, transfer the chilled bark to a cutting board. Using a large chef's knife, coarsely chop the bark into approximate ¼-inch dice. Place the chopped bark in a small bowl and place in the freezer to chill while the ganache continues to cool in the refrigerator.

10 Sprinkle the chopped bark evenly over the ganache in a single layer, then using the back of a metal spatula, lightly tap on the bark to slightly imbed it into the ganache. Refrigerate the pan for 7 to 8 hours, or overnight. See page xii for instructions on removing and cutting the slab, and for refrigerated storage (up to 2 weeks) and freezing guidelines.

don's english toffee almond brownies

As mentioned in my first book, Extreme Brownies: 50 Recipes for the Most Over-the-Top Treats Ever (you already have it, right?) my husband Don loves English toffee, so this brownie was created specifically for him. Fortunately, lots of my customers liked it too, so "Don's" brownie became a hit.

brownie batter

Vegetable shortening for pan
¾ cup (4 ounces) roasted salted almonds
2½ sticks (10 ounces) unsalted butter
¾ cup (4 ounces) 100% cacao unsweetened
  chocolate chips
1¼ cups (7.5 ounces) 63% extra dark chocolate chips
5 large eggs, at room temperature
1¼ cups (8.7 ounces) granulated sugar
1¼ packed cups (10 ounces) light brown sugar
1 teaspoon salt
2 teaspoons pure vanilla extract
1¼ cups (5.6 ounces) unbleached all-purpose flour
½ teaspoon and ⅛ teaspoon baking powder
1 (8-ounce) package English toffee bits, divided (Heath
  Bits O' Brickle)

almond cream cheese frosting

1 (8-ounce) package cream cheese, room temperature
6 tablespoons (3 ounces) unsalted butter, room
  temperature
⅛ teaspoon salt
1½ cups (6 ounces) confectioners' sugar
½ teaspoon ground cinnamon
½ teaspoon pure almond extract

milk chocolate glaze

5 teaspoons (0.07 ounce) canola oil
1½ cups (9 ounces) milk chocolate chips

1   Adjust an oven rack to the middle level of the oven and preheat to 350°F. Prepare a 9 by 13-inch baking pan with heavy-duty aluminum foil as shown on page ix. Lightly grease the foil in the pan.

2   Using a nut chopper or chef's knife, finely chop the almonds. Set aside.

3   To make the brownie batter, cut the butter sticks into ½-inch slices. In a small, heavy saucepan, melt the butter pieces over the lowest setting; add the unsweetened and extra dark chocolate chips. Stir with a small whisk until combined and the chocolate is melted and smooth. Turn off the heat, but leave the saucepan on the burner while proceeding with the recipe.

4   Using a large whisk, lightly beat the eggs in a large mixing bowl. Place the sugars and salt in a separate small mixing bowl, then whisk into the eggs just until

incorporated. Briefly whisk the melted chocolate mixture, then gradually whisk into the egg mixture until just combined. Briefly whisk in the vanilla.

5   Place the flour and baking powder in the small mixing bowl; whisk together to combine. Sift through a medium strainer directly onto the batter; stir in with a silicone spatula until just combined.

6   Set aside ½ cup (3 ounces) of the toffee bits to use later as garnish. Sprinkle the remaining toffee bits and the chopped almonds over the batter and fold in until just combined. Pour the batter into the prepared pan and spread evenly with a small offset spatula. Bake for 34 minutes, until a toothpick inserted in the center of the slab comes out clean. Transfer the pan to a cooling rack set in the freezer to quickly cool the top of the brownie slab before covering it with the almond cream cheese frosting.

7   To make the almond cream cheese frosting, place the cream cheese, butter, and salt in the small mixing bowl. Using a hand mixer on high speed, beat the mixture until it is light and fluffy. Add the confectioners' sugar to the bowl (no need to sift) and beat until creamy and smooth. Add the cinnamon and almond extract and beat in until well combined. Dollop the frosting over the chilled brownie slab and spread evenly with a small offset spatula. Transfer the pan to the refrigerator while preparing the milk chocolate glaze.

8   To make the milk chocolate glaze, bring a medium saucepan with two inches of water just to a boil. Place the canola oil and milk chocolate chips in a metal mixing bowl that will fit over the saucepan to form a double boiler. When the water comes to a boil, take the saucepan off the heat and place the mixing bowl over the hot water: the bottom of the metal bowl should not touch the hot water. Stir with a small silicone spatula until the chocolate is melted

Don's English Toffee
Almond Brownies

and perfectly smooth. Remove the mixing bowl from the saucepan and using a kitchen towel, wipe off any condensation from the bottom of the mixing bowl. Pour the glaze over the almond cream cheese layer. Use a small offset spatula to spread the glaze evenly, then sprinkle the reserved toffee bits evenly over the glaze. Use the back of a metal spatula to lightly tap on the toffee bits to slightly imbed them into the glaze. Refrigerate the pan for 7 to 8 hours, or overnight. See page xii for instructions on removing and cutting the slab, and for refrigerated storage (up to 2 weeks) and freezing guidelines.

walnut bark pudgy brownies

makes 12 large squares or 24 smaller bars

In my first cookbook, Extreme Brownies: 50 Recipes for the Most Over-the-Top Treats Ever, I mentioned that my "Big Fat Walnut Chocolate Chip Brownies" were the brownies most likely to be found in my refrigerator on any given day. Not anymore; this one, with a yummy chocolate marshmallow frosting topped with shards of dark chocolate walnut sea salt bark, has replaced it.

dark chocolate walnut sea salt bark

Vegetable shortening for pan
1/3 cup (1.5 ounces) shelled walnuts
2 teaspoons (0.03 ounce) canola oil
2/3 cup (4 ounces) 63% extra dark chocolate chips
1/2 teaspoon sea salt flakes (Maldon)

brownie batter

Vegetable shortening for pan
2½ sticks (10 ounces) unsalted butter
¾ cup (4 ounces) 100% cacao unsweetened
   chocolate chips
1¼ cups (7.5 ounces) 63% extra dark chocolate chips
5 large eggs, at room temperature
1¼ cups (8.7 ounces) granulated sugar
1¼ packed cups (10 ounces) light brown sugar
1 teaspoon salt
2 teaspoons pure vanilla extract
1¼ cups (5.6 ounces) unbleached all-purpose flour
½ teaspoon and 1/8 teaspoon baking powder
1½ cups (6 ounces) shelled walnuts

chocolate marshmallow frosting

¼ cup and 1 tablespoon (2.5 ounces) 63% extra dark
   chocolate chips

9 tablespoons (4.5 ounces) unsalted butter, at room
   temperature
¼ teaspoon salt
½ teaspoon pure vanilla extract
1 teaspoon chocolate extract
2 cups (8.5 ounces) marshmallow fluff (or creme)
1/3 cup and 4 teaspoons (1.5 ounces) Dutch-processed
   unsweetened cocoa powder

1   To make the dark chocolate sea salt walnut bark, cut out a sheet of parchment paper to line the bottom of a quarter sheet pan. Lightly grease the bottom of the pan and place the parchment paper on top; press down to secure the paper onto the pan. Set aside.

2   Using a nut chopper or chef's knife, finely chop the walnuts. Set aside.

3   Bring a medium saucepan with two inches of water just to a boil. Place the canola oil and chocolate chips in a metal mixing bowl that will fit over the saucepan to form a double boiler. When the water comes to a boil, take the saucepan off the heat and place the

mixing bowl over the hot water: the bottom of the metal bowl should not touch the hot water. Stir with a small silicone spatula until the chocolate is melted and perfectly smooth. Stir in the chopped walnuts. Remove the mixing bowl from the saucepan and using a kitchen towel, wipe off any condensation from the bottom of the mixing bowl. Scrape the mixture onto the parchment-lined pan. Using a small offset spatula, spread the chocolate evenly to about 1/8-inch thickness. Sprinkle the sea salt evenly over the warm chocolate. Refrigerate the pan while proceeding with the recipe.

4   Adjust an oven rack to the middle level of the oven and preheat to 350°F. Prepare a 9 by 13-inch baking pan with heavy-duty aluminum foil as shown on page ix. Lightly grease the foil in the pan.

5   To make the brownie batter, cut the butter sticks into ½-inch slices. In a small, heavy saucepan, melt the butter pieces over the lowest setting; add the unsweetened and extra dark chocolate chips. Stir with a small whisk until combined and the chocolate is melted and smooth. Turn off the heat, but leave the saucepan on the burner while proceeding with the recipe.

6   Using a large whisk, lightly beat the eggs in a large mixing bowl. Place the sugars and salt in a separate small mixing bowl, then whisk into the eggs just until incorporated. Briefly whisk the melted chocolate mixture, then gradually whisk into the egg mixture until just combined. Briefly whisk in the vanilla.

7   Place the flour and baking powder in the small mixing bowl; whisk together to combine. Sift through a medium strainer directly onto the batter; stir in with a silicone spatula until just combined. Sprinkle the walnuts over the batter and fold in until just combined. Pour the batter into the prepared pan and spread evenly with a small offset spatula. Bake for 34

minutes, until a toothpick inserted in the center of the slab comes out clean. Transfer the pan to a cooling rack set in the freezer to quickly cool the slab before covering it with the chocolate marshmallow frosting.

8   To make the chocolate marshmallow frosting, place the chocolate chips in a small heat-proof bowl. Microwave in 30 second intervals, stirring with a small spatula, until the chocolate is melted and smooth. Set aside.

9   Using a stand mixer fitted with the paddle attachment, beat together the butter and salt on medium speed until well combined and completely smooth. Add the extracts and the marshmallow fluff to the mixing bowl and beat on medium-low speed until well combined.

10 Sift or strain the cocoa powder over the mixture and beat in on the lowest speed. Starting on low speed and gradually increasing to medium-high, beat until the frosting is fluffy. Scrape down the sides of the bowl and beat again briefly. Reduce the mixer speed to medium and add the melted chocolate. Increase the speed to medium-high and beat until well combined. Scrape down the sides of the bowl and beat again briefly. Dollop the frosting over the cooled brownie slab. Use a small offset spatula to spread it evenly. If desired, use a pastry comb to created a pattern on the frosting. Place the pan in the refrigerator for 20 minutes to cool down the frosting. Note: Chop the dark chocolate walnut sea salt bark while the frosting is cooling.

11 Using the parchment paper, transfer the chilled bark to a cutting board. Using a large chef's knife, coarsely chop the bark into approximate ½-inch pieces. Place the chopped bark in a small bowl and place in the freezer to chill while the frosting continues to cool in the refrigerator.

Walnut Bark
Pudgy Brownies

12 Sprinkle the chopped bark evenly over the frosting, then using the back of a metal spatula, lightly tap on the bark to slightly imbed it into the frosting. Refrigerate the pan for 7 to 8 hours, or overnight. See page xii for instructions on removing and cutting the slab, and for refrigerated storage (up to 2 weeks) and freezing guidelines.

decadent dark chocolate macadamia nut brownies

makes 12 large squares or 24 smaller bars

Many years ago on a flight we were given a little triangular package of Mauna Loa macadamia nuts. The package had about five nuts inside, and of course I would have liked about five more packages. It truly was a great marketing tool, because on my next shopping trip I bought a jar of Mauna Loa macadamia nuts, which I ate in two sittings. Because of my love of dark chocolate and macadamia nuts, this is one of my favorite brownies that I make quite often for guests.

brownie batter

Vegetable shortening for pan

2½ sticks (10 ounces) unsalted butter

1²/₃ cups (10 ounces) 63% extra dark chocolate chips

5 large eggs, at room temperature

2½ cups (1 pound 1.5 ounces) sugar

1 teaspoon salt

2 teaspoons pure vanilla extract

1 cup (4 ounces) cake flour

1 cup (4 ounces Dutch-processed unsweetened cocoa powder

2 cups (9 ounces) dry roasted macadamia nuts with sea salt

dark chocolate frosting

¾ cup and 1 tablespoon (5.3 ounces) 60% cacao bittersweet chocolate chips

11 tablespoons (6.5 ounces) unsalted butter, at room temperature

¹/₈ teaspoon salt

¾ scant cup (2.7 ounces) confectioners' sugar

½ cup (2 ounces) Dutch-processed unsweetened cocoa powder

½ cup (6 ounces) light corn syrup

½ teaspoon chocolate extract

¼ teaspoon pure vanilla extract

garnish

½ cup (2 ounces) dry roasted macadamia nuts with sea salt

1   Adjust an oven rack to the middle level of the oven and preheat to 350°F. Prepare a 9 by 13-inch baking pan with heavy-duty aluminum foil as shown on page ix. Lightly grease the foil in the pan.

2   To make the brownie batter, cut the butter sticks into ½-inch slices. In a small, heavy saucepan, begin to melt the butter pieces over the lowest setting; add the extra dark chocolate chips. Stir with a small whisk

until combined and the chocolate is melted and smooth. Turn off the heat, but leave the saucepan on the burner while proceeding with the recipe.

3   Using a large whisk, lightly beat the eggs in a large mixing bowl. Place the sugar and salt in a separate small mixing bowl, then whisk into the eggs just until incorporated. Briefly whisk the melted chocolate mixture, then gradually whisk into the egg mixture until just combined. Briefly whisk in the vanilla.

4   Place the flour and cocoa powder in the small mixing bowl; whisk together to combine. Sift through a medium strainer directly onto the batter; stir in with a silicone spatula until just combined. Pour a scant half (1 pound 9 ounces) of the brownie batter into the prepared pan. The best way to do this is by weight. Place the prepared pan on a scale, tare off (subtract)

the weight of the pan, and scrape the correct weight of batter directly into the pan. Spread the batter evenly with a small offset spatula. Sprinkle the macadamia nuts evenly over the batter. Dollop the remaining brownie batter over the nuts and spread evenly with a small offset spatula, taking care to cover the nuts completely. Bake for 34 minutes, until a toothpick inserted in the center of the slab comes out clean. Transfer the pan to a cooling rack set in the freezer to quickly cool the top of the brownie slab before covering it with the dark chocolate frosting.

5   To make the dark chocolate frosting, place the bittersweet chocolate chips in a 1-cup Pyrex measuring cup. Microwave the chips on high power for 90 seconds, then stir the chocolate chips with a small silicone spatula until the chips are almost melted. Microwave the chips on high for an additional 15 seconds and stir until the chips are completely melted and smooth. Set aside.

Decadent Dark Chocolate
Macadamia Nut Brownies

6   Cut the butter into ¼-inch slices. Place the butter and salt in the bowl of a stand mixer fitted with the paddle attachment. Beat on medium-high speed while continuing with the recipe.

7   Place the confectioners' sugar and cocoa in the small mixing bowl; whisk together to combine. Remove the mixer bowl and paddle from the mixer stand. Sift the sugar/cocoa mixture through a medium strainer directly onto the butter in the mixer bowl. Return the bowl and paddle to the mixer stand and beat on low speed until the mixture is combined and forms a thick chocolate paste.

8   Add the corn syrup: the best way to do this is by weight. Place the mixer bowl and paddle on a scale, tare off (subtract) the weight. Add the corn syrup directly into the mixer bowl onto the frosting mixture. Return the mixer bowl and paddle back to the mixer stand, and on medium-low speed, beat in the corn syrup. On low speed, add the extracts. Scrape down the sides of the bowl with a medium silicone spatula and beat again briefly.

9   With the mixer on medium-low speed, add the melted chocolate and beat until just combined. Scrape down the sides of the bowl and beat again briefly. Dollop the frosting over the cooled brownie slab and spread evenly with a small offset spatula. If desired, use a pastry comb to create a decorative design on the frosting.

10   To make the garnish, chop the macadamia nuts using a nut grinder, or chop by hand using a large chef's knife. Sprinkle the chopped nuts evenly over the soft frosting, then use the back of a metal spatula to lightly tap on the nuts to slightly imbed them into the frosting. Refrigerate the pan for 7 to 8 hours, or overnight. See page xii for instructions on removing and cutting the slab, and for refrigerated storage (up to 2 weeks) and freezing guidelines.

bullwinkle the mousse brownies

makes 12 large squares or 24 smaller bars

Don't let the name fool you: this is the most elegant brownie in this book. I helped put my husband Don through college making chocolate mousse cakes for The Balcony restaurant in Pittsburgh, which is sadly, long gone. With this dessert, the mousse part of that dessert lives on.

brownie batter

Vegetable shortening for pan
1½ sticks (6 ounces) unsalted butter
1/3 cup (2 ounces) 100% cacao unsweetened
   chocolate chips
¾ cup and 1 tablespoon (5 ounces) 63% extra dark
   chocolate chips
3 large eggs, at room temperature
¾ cup (5.3 ounces) granulated sugar
¾ packed cup (6 ounces) light brown sugar
¾ teaspoon salt
1½ teaspoons pure vanilla extract
¾ cup (3.4 ounces) unbleached all-purpose flour
½ teaspoon baking powder

chocolate mousse

2 cups (12 ounces) *semi-sweet chocolate chips
   (Hershey's)
4 large eggs, at room temperature
12 ounces (1½ cups) heavy whipping cream
¼ cup (1 ounce) confectioners' sugar
*Don't be tempted to use a chocolate with a higher cacao
   content: it will become too thick of a mass when the
   eggs and egg yolks are added.

mascarpone chantilly

8 ounces mascarpone cheese
1 cup (8 ounces) heavy whipping cream
¼ cup (1.8 ounces) sugar
1 teaspoon vanilla bean paste (or pure vanilla extract)

garnish

½ teaspoon Dutch-processed unsweetened
   cocoa powder

1   Adjust an oven rack to the middle level of the oven and preheat to 350°F. Prepare a 9 by 13-inch baking pan with heavy-duty aluminum foil as shown on page ix. Lightly grease the foil in the pan.

2   Cut out a sheet of parchment paper to measure 9½ x 13½ inches. Lightly grease the bottom and interior sides of a 9 by 13-inch baking pan with a removable bottom. Place the parchment paper on the bottom of the pan to come ¼-inch up the sides of the pan. Lightly grease the parchment paper. Set aside. Note: If you don't have a pan with a removable bottom, prepare the pan with foil as directed on page ix. Because of the Mascarpone Chantilly topping, you

cannot "flip" the slab out, but you can cut squares out of the pan and lift them out with a spatula.

3   To make the brownie batter, cut the butter sticks into ½-inch slices. In a small, heavy saucepan, melt the butter pieces over the lowest setting; add the unsweetened and extra dark chocolate chips. Stir with a small whisk until combined and the chocolate is melted and smooth. Turn off the heat, but leave the saucepan on the burner while proceeding with the recipe.

4   Using a large whisk, lightly beat the eggs in a large mixing bowl. Place the sugars and salt in a separate small mixing bowl, then whisk into the eggs just until incorporated. Briefly whisk the melted chocolate mixture, then gradually whisk into the egg mixture until just combined. Briefly whisk in the vanilla.

5   Place the flour and baking powder in the small mixing bowl; whisk together to combine. Sift through a medium strainer directly onto the batter; stir in with a silicone spatula until just combined. Pour the batter into the prepared pan and spread evenly with a small offset spatula. Bake for 23 minutes, until a toothpick inserted in the center of the slab comes out clean. Transfer the pan to a cooling rack set in the freezer to quickly cool the top of the brownie slab before covering it with the chocolate mousse.

6   To make the chocolate mousse, bring a medium saucepan with two inches of water just to a simmer. Place the chocolate chips in a metal mixing bowl that will fit over the saucepan to form a double boiler: the bottom of the metal bowl should not touch the simmering water. Stir the chocolate chips occasionally with a silicone spatula until the chocolate is melted. When the chips are completely melted and smooth, remove the saucepan from the heat, but keep the bowl with the melted chocolate in place over the saucepan with water to keep the chocolate warm.

7   Place 3 egg whites (reserving the egg yolks in a small bowl) in the metal bowl of a stand mixer fitted with the whisk attachment. Place the whole egg in a separate small bowl. Set aside.

8   Place the heavy cream and confectioners' sugar in a small mixing bowl. Using a hand mixer starting on medium and gradually increasing to high, beat together just until soft peaks form. Set aside.

9   Remove the metal mixing bowl from the top of the saucepan with water and carefully dry the bottom of the metal mixing bowl with a towel. Using a silicone spatula, scrape the melted chocolate into a large plastic mixing bowl. Using a silicone spatula, add the whole egg to the melted chocolate and mix very well, stirring very rapidly. Add the 3 egg yolks and beat rapidly with the spatula until the chocolate mixture is completely blended and smooth. Dollop about half of the whipped cream over the melted chocolate and stir in with the spatula to lighten the mixture. Set aside.

10 Begin to beat the egg whites on low speed. Gradually increase the mixer speed to high and beat until the whites are glossy and very stiff, but not dry. Dollop the beaten egg whites and the remaining whipped cream over the chocolate mixture and fold in with the spatula just until blended. Dollop the mousse over the chilled brownie slab. Use a small offset spatula to smooth the top. Refrigerate the pan for at least 6 hours before removing the slab from the pan and covering it with the mascarpone chantilly.

11 After the brownie slab is well chilled, run a small knife around the edges of the brownie slab. Carefully push the bottom of the pan up out of the pan sides and place the chilled brownie slab (still on the parchment-lined bottom) on a cutting board.

12 Fit a medium (14-inch) pastry bag with a 3/8-inch round plain pastry tip (Ateco #804). Set aside.

13 To make the mascarpone chantilly, combine the mascarpone, heavy cream, sugar, and vanilla bean paste in a stand mixer bowl fitted with the whisk attachment. Starting on low speed and gradually increasing to high, beat until soft peaks form: be careful not to overbeat. Load the chantilly into the prepared bag. Pipe horizontal rows of the chantilly over the slab, completely covering the mousse. Sift the cocoa powder through a fine-mesh strainer over the chantilly. Chill the slab (still on the cutting board) for at least 1 hour more before cutting. See page xii for instructions on cutting the slab, and for refrigerated storage (up to 1 week) and freezing guidelines.

Bullwinkle The Mousse Brownies

samoa brownies

makes 12 large squares or 24 smaller bars

When girl scouts start selling their cookies, I am on the prowl for a box (or four) of their yummy Samoa cookies. This brownie is my ode to Samoas, as well as a salute to all dedicated girl and boy scouts everywhere.

coconut for the caramel-coconut layer
1½ cups (4.2 ounces) organic unsweetened shredded coconut (Let's Do Organic)

brownie batter
3 sticks (12 ounces) unsalted butter
2 cups (12 ounces) 63% extra dark chocolate chips
6 large eggs, at room temperature
3 cups (1 pound 5 ounces) sugar
1¼ teaspoons salt
1 tablespoon pure vanilla extract
1¼ cups (5 ounces) cake flour
1 cup and 2 tablespoons (4.2 ounces) Dutch-processed unsweetened cocoa powder

caramel-coconut layer
$1/3$ cup and 1 teaspoon (3 ounces) heavy whipping cream
2 tablespoons (1 ounce) unsalted butter
12 ounces (about 41) caramel candies (Kraft Traditional Caramels)
1 teaspoon pure vanilla extract

chocolate drizzle
2 tablespoons (1 ounce) unsalted butter
2 teaspoons (0.04 ounce) light corn syrup
½ cup (3 ounces) Special Dark chocolate chips (Nestle's)
1½ teaspoons very hot water

1   Adjust an oven rack to the middle level of the oven and preheat to 350°F. Prepare a 9 by 13-inch baking pan with heavy-duty aluminum foil as shown on page ix. Lightly grease the foil in the pan.

2   Spread the unsweetened coconut out evenly onto a half-sheet pan. Bake for 4 to 5 minutes; the coconut should be a uniform golden-brown color. Transfer the pan to a cooling rack to use later in the caramel-coconut topping. Maintain the oven temperature at 350°F.

3   To make the brownie batter, cut the butter sticks into ½-inch slices. In a small, heavy saucepan, begin to melt the butter pieces over the lowest setting; add the extra dark chocolate chips. Stir with a small whisk until combined and the chocolate is melted and smooth. Turn off the heat, but leave the saucepan on the burner while proceeding with the recipe.

4   Using a large whisk, lightly beat the eggs in a large mixing bowl. Place the sugar and salt in a separate small mixing bowl, then whisk into the eggs just until incorporated. Briefly whisk the melted chocolate mixture, then gradually whisk into the egg mixture until just combined. Briefly whisk in the vanilla.

5   Place the flour and cocoa powder in the small mixing bowl; whisk together to combine. Sift through a medium strainer directly onto the batter; stir in with a silicone spatula until just combined. Pour the batter into the prepared pan and spread evenly with a small offset spatula. Bake for 36 minutes, until a toothpick inserted in the center of the slab comes out clean. Transfer the pan to a cooling rack. Note: Make the caramel-coconut layer while the brownie slab is baking.

6   To make the caramel-coconut layer, cut the butter into ¼-inch slices. Place the butter slices and cream in a 2-quart saucier or saucepan. Begin to melt the mixture over very low heat. Unwrap the caramels, and as each is unwrapped, add it to the mixture. Cook over medium-low heat, stirring occasionally with a silicone spatula, until the caramels are melted and completely smooth. Stir in the vanilla.

7   Sprinkle 2.8 ounces (1 cup) of the toasted coconut over the caramel and stir in. Dollop the mixture over the brownie slab and spread evenly with a small offset spatula. Sprinkle the remaining coconut evenly over the top of the caramel layer, then tap it lightly with the back of a metal spatula to slightly embed the coconut into the caramel. Refrigerate the pan for 7 to 8 hours, or overnight.

8   After the slab has been well chilled, see page xii for instructions on removing and cutting the slab into 12 large squares. Place six of the brownie squares close together on a piece of parchment paper.

9   To make the chocolate drizzle, melt the butter and corn syrup over low heat in a small, heavy saucepan. Remove the pan from the heat and add the chocolate chips; stir with a small silicone spatula until the chocolate is melted and smooth. Stir in the hot water to thin out. Pour the chocolate mixture into a medium (12-ounce) plastic squeeze bottle. Note: Instead of using a plastic bottle, the spatula can be used to randomly drizzle the melted chocolate over the brownies.

10 Using the plastic bottle, squeeze parallel lines on the diagonal about ¼-inch apart over the top of the brownies. Transfer the drizzled brownies to a sheet of parchment paper-lined half-sheet pan. Continue in the same manner with the remaining six brownies, then chill the brownies on the sheet pan for 15 minutes to set up the chocolate. See page xiv for refrigerated storage (up to 2 weeks) and freezing guidelines.

Samoa Brownies

crispy caramel nougat brownies

makes 12 large squares or 24 smaller bars

When I buy cereal these days, it's not to pour in a bowl with ice cold milk (and copious amounts of sugar) for breakfast. No, the cereals I buy now are to enhance a baked good or chocolate bark with a delicious, textural crunch.

---

brownie batter
Vegetable shortening for pan
2½ sticks (10 ounces) unsalted butter
1²/₃ cups (10 ounces) 63% extra dark chocolate chips
5 large eggs, at room temperature
2½ cups (1 pound 1.5 ounces) sugar
1 teaspoon salt
2 teaspoons pure vanilla extract
1 cup (4 ounces) cake flour
1 cup (4 ounces Dutch-processed unsweetened
   cocoa powder

caramel nougat
7.2 ounces (1½ cups) marshmallow fluff or crème
¾ cup (4 ounces) sea salt caramel baking chips
4 tablespoons (2 ounces) unsalted butter
1 cup (7 ounces) granulated sugar
¼ cup (2.2 ounces) evaporated milk
¼ teaspoon salt
1 teaspoon caramel flavor
½ teaspoon pure vanilla extract
1½ cups (1.2 ounces) sweetened toasted rice cereal
   (Frosted Krispies)

chocolate glaze
6 tablespoons (3 ounces) unsalted butter
1 tablespoon (0.08 ounce) light corn syrup
1 cup (6 ounces) 60% cacao bittersweet chocolate chips

garnish
¾ teaspoon sea salt flakes (Maldon)

1   Adjust an oven rack to the middle level of the oven and preheat to 350°F. Prepare a 9 by 13-inch baking pan with heavy-duty aluminum foil as shown on page ix. Lightly grease the foil in the pan.

2   To make the brownie batter, cut the butter sticks into ½-inch slices. In a small, heavy saucepan, begin to melt the butter pieces over the lowest setting; add the extra dark chocolate chips. Stir with a small whisk until combined and the chocolate is melted and smooth. Turn off the heat, but leave the saucepan on the burner while proceeding with the recipe.

3   Using a large whisk, lightly beat the eggs in a large mixing bowl. Place the sugar and salt in a separate small mixing bowl, then whisk into the eggs just until incorporated. Briefly whisk the melted chocolate mixture, then gradually whisk into the egg mixture until just combined. Briefly whisk in the vanilla. Note: Set aside the saucepan and small whisk (no need to wash them) to use later for the chocolate glaze.

4   Place the flour and cocoa powder in the small mixing bowl; whisk together to combine. Sift through a medium strainer directly onto the batter; stir in with a silicone spatula until just combined. Pour the batter into the prepared pan and spread evenly with a small offset spatula. Bake for 34 minutes, until a toothpick inserted in the center of the slab comes out clean. Transfer the pan to a cooling rack set in the refrigerator.

5   To make the caramel nougat, place the fluff in a small bowl; set aside. Place the caramel chips in a separate small bowl; set aside.

6   Cut the butter into ¼-inch thick slices. Place the butter, sugar, and evaporated milk in a medium (1½ to 2-quart) saucepan. Cook over medium-low heat, stirring occasionally with a silicone spatula, until the butter is melted and the sugar is dissolved. Increase the heat to medium-high and bring the mixture to a boil, then reduce the heat to the lowest setting and boil for 5 minutes, occasionally stirring the mixture to prevent the bottom from scorching. Remove the pan from the heat and stir in the salt, fluff, and caramel chips, stirring vigorously until the mixture is well blended and the caramel chips are melted and smooth. Stir in the caramel flavor and vanilla. Pour the nougat over the brownie slab and spread evenly with a small offset spatula. Sprinkle the cereal evenly over the caramel nougat layer, then tap the cereal lightly with the back of a metal spatula to imbed it slightly into the nougat.

7   To make the chocolate glaze, slice the butter into ¼-inch slices. Place the butter slices and corn syrup in the reserved small saucepan and melt over the lowest setting. Meanwhile, place the chocolate chips in a 2-cup Pyrex measuring cup. Microwave the chips on high power for 90 seconds, whisk with the reserved small whisk, then microwave an additional 15 seconds: whisk again. Pour the melted butter mixture into the melted chocolate and whisk gently until combined and completely smooth. Pour the glaze over the caramel nougat layer and spread evenly with a small offset spatula, then sprinkle the sea salt over the glaze. Refrigerate the pan for 7 to 8 hours, or overnight. See page xii for instructions on removing and cutting the slab, and for refrigerated storage (up to 2 weeks) and freezing guidelines.

Crispy Caramel
Nougat Brownies

cheeky sour cherry brownies

makes 12 large squares or 24 smaller bars

If you love chocolate covered cherries (like my husband Don does) then this is the brownie for you. It shot up the list of customer favorites as soon as I trotted it out, and I know quite a few people who will be very happy that now they can make it too. Don't be alarmed if the cherry fluff frosting ends up with a few visible pieces of cherries in it from the cherry spread; I think they're kind of cool.

brownie batter
Vegetable shortening for pan
1 (5-ounce) package dried tart cherries (Stoneridge Orchards)
1 teaspoon canola oil
2½ sticks (10 ounces) unsalted butter
¾ cup (4 ounces) 100% cacao unsweetened chocolate chips
1¼ cups (7.5 ounces) 63% extra dark chocolate chips
5 large eggs, at room temperature
1¼ cups (8.7 ounces) granulated sugar
1¼ packed cups (10 ounces) light brown sugar
1 teaspoon salt
2 teaspoons pure vanilla extract
1¼ cups (5.6 ounces) unbleached all-purpose flour
½ teaspoon and $1/8$ teaspoon baking powder

cherry fluff frosting
¼ cup (1.6 ounces) white all-vegetable shortening
4 tablespoons (2 ounces) unsalted butter, at room temperature
2 tablespoons (1.5 ounces) *sour cherry spread (Dalmatia)
½ teaspoon cherry extract
1¼ cups (6 ounces) marshmallow fluff (or creme)
¼ cup (1 ounce) confectioners' sugar

*Alternately, substitute sour cherry jam

chocolate glaze
6 tablespoons (3 ounces) unsalted butter
1 tablespoon (0.08 ounce) light corn syrup
1 cup (6 ounces) 60% cacao bittersweet chocolate chips

garnish
½ cup (2 ounces) roasted salted whole almonds

1   Adjust an oven rack to the middle level of the oven and preheat to 350°F. Prepare a 9 by 13-inch baking pan with heavy-duty aluminum foil as shown on page ix. Lightly grease the foil in the pan.

2   Place the tart cherries in the small mixing bowl; add the canola oil. Toss the cherries and canola oil together to coat the cherries; having a bit of oil on the cherries makes them stick less to the blade of your knife as you chop. Turn the cherries out onto a cutting board and coarsely chop them with a large chef's knife. Set aside.

3   To make the brownie batter, cut the butter sticks into ½-inch slices. In a small, heavy saucepan, melt the butter pieces over the lowest setting; add the unsweetened and extra dark chocolate chips. Stir with a small whisk until combined and the chocolate is melted and smooth. Turn off the heat, but leave the saucepan on the burner while proceeding with the recipe.

4   Using a large whisk, lightly beat the eggs in a large mixing bowl. Place the sugars and salt in a separate small mixing bowl, then whisk into the eggs just until incorporated. Briefly whisk the melted chocolate mixture, then gradually whisk into the egg mixture until just combined. Briefly whisk in the vanilla. Note: Set aside the saucepan and small whisk (no need to wash them) to use later for the chocolate glaze.

5   Place the flour and baking powder in the small mixing bowl; whisk together to combine. Sift through a medium strainer directly onto the batter; stir in with a silicone spatula until just combined. Sprinkle the chopped cherries over the batter and fold in until just combined. Pour the batter into the prepared pan and spread evenly with a small offset spatula. Bake for 34 minutes, until a toothpick inserted in the center of the slab comes out clean. Transfer the pan to a cooling rack set in the freezer to quickly cool the top of the brownie slab before covering it with the cherry fluff frosting.

6   To make the cherry fluff frosting, using a stand mixer fitted with the paddle attachment, beat together the shortening and butter on medium speed until well combined. Add the cherry spread, cherry extract, and marshmallow fluff to the mixing bowl and beat on medium-low speed until well combined. Add the confectioners' sugar (no need to sift) to the mixer bowl. Starting on low speed and gradually increasing to medium-high, beat until the mixture is fluffy, about 1 minute. Dollop the frosting over the chilled brownie slab and spread evenly with a small offset spatula. Transfer the pan to the refrigerator while preparing the chocolate glaze.

7   To make the chocolate glaze, slice the butter into ¼-inch slices. Place the butter slices and corn syrup in the reserved small saucepan and melt over the lowest setting. Meanwhile, place the chocolate chips in a 2-cup Pyrex measuring cup. Microwave the chips on high power for 90 seconds, whisk with the reserved small whisk, then microwave an additional 15 seconds: whisk again. Pour the melted butter mixture into the melted chocolate and whisk gently until combined and completely smooth. Pour the glaze over the cherry fluff frosting and spread evenly with a small offset spatula.

8   To make the garnish, using a nut chopper or chef's knife, finely chop the almonds. Sprinkle the chopped almonds evenly over the warm glaze. Refrigerate the pan for 7 to 8 hours, or overnight. See page xii for instructions on removing and cutting the slab, and for refrigerated storage (up to 2 weeks) and freezing guidelines.

Cheeky Sour
Cherry Brownies

stuffed strawberry bark brownies

makes 12 large squares or 24 smaller bars

You may wonder why I make barks to use in and on my brownies. Basically, I am creating my own candy bars. Believe me, I tried to find a white chocolate strawberry candy bar and had no luck. I have had such fun creating delicious barks, that sometimes I make them to cut up in large chunks to package in small glassine bags as gifts for friends.

crispy white chocolate strawberry bark
Vegetable shortening for pan
½ cup (0.03 ounce) unsweetened freeze dried strawberries (Trader Joe's)
½ cup (0.05 ounce) sweetened toasted rice cereal (Frosted Krispies)
1 tablespoon (0.04 ounce) canola oil
6 ounces white chocolate (from two Lindt 4.4-ounce candy bars)

brownie batter
Vegetable shortening for pan
2½ sticks (10 ounces) unsalted butter
¾ cup (4 ounces) 100% cacao unsweetened chocolate chips
1¼ cups (7.5 ounces) 63% extra dark chocolate chips
5 large eggs, at room temperature
1¼ cups (8.7 ounces) granulated sugar
1¼ packed cups (10 ounces) light brown sugar
1 teaspoon salt
2 teaspoons pure vanilla extract
1¼ cups (5.6 ounces) unbleached all-purpose flour
½ teaspoon and ⅛ teaspoon baking powder
1 (12 to 14-ounce) jar strawberry fruit spread or jam

chocolate glaze
6 tablespoons (3 ounces) unsalted butter
1 tablespoon (0.08 ounce) light corn syrup
1 cup (6 ounces) 60% cacao bittersweet chocolate chip

garnish
2 tablespoons strawberry crispearls

1   To make the crispy white chocolate strawberry bark, cut out a sheet of parchment paper to line the bottom of a quarter sheet pan. Lightly grease the bottom of the pan and place the parchment paper on top; press down to secure the paper onto the pan.

2   Using a chef's knife, coarsely chop the freeze-dried strawberries and place in a small bowl; add the cereal. Set aside.

3   Finely chop the white chocolate. Set aside.

4   Bring a medium saucepan with two inches of water just to a boil. Place the canola oil and chopped white chocolate in a metal mixing bowl that will fit over the

saucepan to form a double boiler. When the water comes to a boil, take the saucepan off the heat and place the mixing bowl over the hot water: the bottom of the metal bowl should not touch the hot water. Stir with a small silicone spatula until the white chocolate is melted and perfectly smooth. Stir in the chopped strawberries and rice cereal. Remove the mixing bowl from the saucepan and using a kitchen towel, wipe off any condensation from the bottom of the mixing bowl. Scrape the mixture onto the parchment-lined pan. Using a small offset spatula, spread the white chocolate evenly to about ¼-inch thickness. Refrigerate the pan while proceeding with the recipe. Note: Set aside the saucepan and small whisk (no need to wash them) to use later for the chocolate glaze.

5   Adjust an oven rack to the middle level of the oven and preheat to 350°F. Prepare a 9 by 13-inch baking pan with heavy-duty aluminum foil as shown on page ix. Lightly grease the foil in the pan.

6   To make the brownie batter, cut the butter sticks into ½-inch slices. In a small, heavy saucepan, begin to melt the butter pieces over the lowest setting; add the unsweetened and extra dark chocolate chips. Stir with a small whisk until combined and the chocolate is melted and smooth. Turn off the heat, but leave the saucepan on the burner while proceeding with the recipe.

7   Using a large whisk, lightly beat the eggs in a large mixing bowl. Place the sugars and salt in a separate small mixing bowl, then whisk into the eggs just until incorporated. Briefly whisk the melted chocolate mixture, then gradually whisk into the egg mixture until just combined. Briefly whisk in the vanilla.

8   Place the flour and baking powder in the small mixing bowl; whisk together to combine. Sift through a medium strainer directly onto the batter; stir in with

a silicone spatula until just combined. Pour half (1 pound 10 ounces) of the brownie batter into the prepared pan. The best way to do this is by weight. Place the prepared pan on a scale, tare off (subtract) the weight of the pan, and scrape the correct weight of batter directly into the pan. Spread the batter evenly with a small offset spatula. Bake for 16 minutes, until a toothpick inserted in the center of the slab comes out clean.

9   After the bottom brownie layer has baked for 16 minutes, transfer the pan to a cooling rack. Dollop the strawberry spread over the hot brownie base. Using a small offset spatula, spread it evenly to within ¼-inch of the outer edges of the pan. Dollop the remaining brownie batter evenly over the strawberry spread and carefully spread to the edges with the offset spatula, covering the strawberry spread. Return the pan to the oven and bake an additional 27 minutes, until a toothpick inserted in the center of the slab comes out clean. Transfer the pan to a cooling rack.

10 To make the chocolate glaze, slice the butter into ¼-inch slices. Place the butter slices and corn syrup in the reserved small saucepan and melt over the lowest setting. Meanwhile, place the chocolate chips in a 2-cup Pyrex measuring cup. Microwave the chips on high power for 90 seconds, whisk with the reserved small whisk, then microwave an additional 15 seconds: whisk again. Pour the melted butter mixture into the melted chocolate and whisk gently until combined and completely smooth. Pour the glaze over the warm brownie slab and spread evenly with a small offset spatula. Place the pan in the refrigerator for 20 minutes to cool down the glaze. Note: Chop the crispy white chocolate strawberry bark while the glaze is cooling.

11 Using the parchment paper, transfer the chilled bark to a cutting board. Using a large chef's knife, coarsely

chop the bark into approixmate ¼-inch dice. Place the chopped bark in a small bowl and place in the freezer to chill while the glaze continues to cool in the refrigerator.

12 Sprinkle the chopped bark evenly over the glaze in a single layer. Sprinkle the strawberry crispearls randomly over and around the bark, then using the back of a metal spatula, lightly tap on the bark pieces and crispearls to slightly imbed them into the glaze. Refrigerate the pan for 7 to 8 hours, or overnight. See page xii for instructions on removing and cutting the slab, and for refrigerated storage (up to 1 week) and freezing guidelines.

Stuffed Strawberry
Bark Brownies

romantic raspberry truffle brownies

I don't know why people always serve strawberries on Valentine's Day. Where I live, they are hard, dry, and tasteless at that time of year. For me, this elegant brownie is the perfect ending for a romantic Valentine's Day dinner. If you can't find the Ghirardelli Dark Chocolate Raspberry Radiance candy bars, omit them and increase the extra dark chocolate chips from 4 ounces to 10 ounces. You will still use 2 ounces of unsweetened chocolate chips. Heart-shaped candies, used for garnish, are only available around Valentine's Day, so stock up if you want to make this brownie other times of the year.

brownie batter
Vegetable shortening for pan
1 (6 ounce) container fresh raspberries
2½ sticks (10 ounces) unsalted butter
2 (3.5-ounces each) Ghirardelli Dark Chocolate Raspberry Radiance candy bars
1/3 cup (2 ounces) 100% cacao unsweetened chocolate chips
2/3 cup (4 ounces) 63% extra dark chocolate chips
5 large eggs, at room temperature
1¼ cups (8.7 ounces) granulated sugar
1¼ packed cups (10 ounces) light brown sugar
1 teaspoon salt
2 teaspoons pure vanilla extract
1¼ cups (5.6 ounces) unbleached all-purpose flour
½ teaspoon and 1/8 teaspoon baking powder

shiny chocolate ganache
1 cup (6 ounces) semisweet chocolate chips
2/3 cup (4 ounces) milk chocolate chips
4 teaspoons (0.06 ounce) unsalted butter
½ cup and 2 tablespoons (5 ounces) heavy whipping cream

garnish
2-3 tablespoons Dutch-processed unsweetened cocoa powder

optional garnish
Heart shaped chocolate candy (Ghirardelli)

1 Adjust an oven rack to the middle level of the oven and preheat to 350°F. Prepare a 9 by 13-inch baking pan with heavy-duty aluminum foil as shown on page ix. Lightly grease the foil in the pan.

2 Place the raspberries on a quarter-sheet pan, individually spaced apart. Place the pan in the freezer.

3 To make the brownie batter, cut the butter sticks into ½-inch slices. In a small, heavy saucepan, begin to melt the butter pieces over the lowest setting. While the butter is melting, chop the candy bars into ½-inch pieces; add the chopped candy bar pieces to the melting butter along with the unsweetened and extra dark chocolate chips. Stir with a small whisk until combined and the chocolate is melted and smooth. Turn off the heat, but leave the saucepan on the burner while proceeding with the recipe.

4 Using a large whisk, lightly beat the eggs in a large mixing bowl. Place the sugars and salt in a separate small mixing bowl, then whisk into the eggs just until incorporated. Briefly whisk the melted chocolate mixture, then gradually whisk into the egg mixture until just combined. Briefly whisk in the vanilla. Note: Set aside the saucepan and small whisk (no need to wash them) to use later for the chocolate ganache.

5 Place the flour and baking powder in the small mixing bowl; whisk together to combine. Sift through a medium strainer directly onto the batter; stir in with a silicone spatula until just combined. Pour a scant half (1 pound 8 ounces) of the batter into the prepared pan. The best way to do this is by weight. Place the prepared pan on a scale, tare off (subtract) the weight of the pan, and scrape the correct weight of batter directly into the pan. Spread the batter evenly with a small offset spatula. Place the frozen raspberries evenly over the batter, pushing them

down into the batter. Dollop the remaining brownie batter over the raspberries and spread evenly with a small offset spatula, taking care to completely cover the raspberries. Bake for 40 minutes, until a toothpick inserted in the center comes out clean. Transfer the pan to a cooling rack.

6 To make the shiny chocolate ganache, place the semisweet and the milk chocolate chips in a small bowl; set aside. Cut the butter into tiny (1/8-inch) dice; set aside.

7 Bring the cream just to a simmer over medium-high heat in the reserved saucepan. Remove the pan from the heat and add the chocolate chips; shake the pan to cover the chips with the hot cream. Cover the pan tightly and let sit off the heat for 2 minutes.

8 Add the butter bits, then place the pan back on the burner (heat turned off) and gently blend the mixture together with a small whisk just until the chips and butter are melted and incorporated into a shiny, smooth ganache. Pour the ganache over the warm slab and spread evenly with a small offset spatula. Refrigerate the pan for 7 to 8 hours, or overnight.

9 Remove the brownie slab from the pan as illustrated on page xii. Peel off and discard the foil and place the slab on a cutting board. Using a medium strainer, sift the cocoa powder to evenly cover the top of the slab. Note: For the best look, use a high-quality unsweetened cocoa powder, like Valrhona.

10 See page xii for instructions on cutting the slab. Cut the slab into 12 large squares. If desired, place a heart-shaped candy in the center of each square. See page xiv for refrigerated storage (up to 5 days) and freezing guidelines.

Romantic Raspberry
Truffle Brownies

bananarama brownies

makes 12 large squares or 24 smaller bars

I am a passionate, if not particularly skillful, tennis player. I have the pleasure of partnering with a retired doctor named Dom. My name is Connie, so we are "Team Condom." I told Dom I'd like to create a brownie with him in mind, and asked what he liked to eat. He said every day he has a banana for breakfast, so Dom, this brownie was created with you in mind. Now if we could just win on a more regular basis...

brownie batter

Vegetable shortening for pan
2 sticks (8 ounces) unsalted butter
½ cup (3 ounces) 100% cacao unsweetened
    chocolate chips
1 cup (6 ounces) 63% extra dark chocolate chips
4 large eggs, at room temperature
1 cup (7 ounces) granulated sugar
1 packed cup (8 ounces) light brown sugar
¾ teaspoon salt
1½ teaspoons pure vanilla extract
1 cup (4.5 ounces) unbleached all-purpose flour
½ teaspoon baking powder
3 large, barely ripe bananas

roasted banana cream cheese frosting

1 small, ripe, banana
1 (8-ounce) package cream cheese, at room temperature
6 tablespoons (3 ounces) unsalted butter, at
    room temperature
½ teaspoon salt
¼ teaspoon pure vanilla extract
2 cups (8 ounces) confectioners' sugar

chocolate glaze

6 tablespoons (3 ounces) unsalted butter
1 tablespoon (0.08 ounce) light corn syrup
1 cup (6 ounces) 60% cacao bittersweet chocolate chips

garnish

¼ cup (0.04 ounce) baked crunchy banana chips (Bare)

1   Adjust an oven rack to the middle level of the oven and preheat to 350°F. Prepare a 9 by 13-inch baking pan with heavy-duty aluminum foil as shown on page ix. Lightly grease the foil in the pan.

2   To make the brownie batter, cut the butter sticks into ½-inch slices. In a small, heavy saucepan, begin to melt the butter pieces over the lowest setting; add the unsweetened and extra dark chocolate chips. Stir with a small whisk until combined and the chocolate is melted and smooth. Turn off the heat, but leave the saucepan on the burner while proceeding with the recipe.

3   Using a large whisk, lightly beat the eggs in a large mixing bowl. Place the sugars and salt in a separate small mixing bowl, then whisk into the eggs just until incorporated. Briefly whisk the melted chocolate mixture, then gradually whisk into the egg mixture until just combined. Briefly whisk in the vanilla. Note: Set aside the saucepan and small whisk (no need to wash them) to use later for the chocolate glaze.

4   Place the flour and baking powder in the small mixing bowl; whisk together to combine. Sift through a medium strainer directly onto the batter; stir in with a silicone spatula until just combined. Pour a scant half (1 pound 3 ounces) of the brownie batter into the prepared pan. The best way to do this is by weight. Place the prepared pan on a scale, tare off (subtract) the weight of the pan, and scrape the correct weight of batter directly into the pan. Spread the batter evenly with a small offset spatula.

5   Slice the bananas on the diagonal into ¼-inch thick slices. Position the banana slices evenly over the batter. Dollop the remaining batter over the banana slices and spread it evenly with a small offset spatula. Bake for 30 minutes, until a toothpick inserted in the center of the slab comes out clean. Transfer the pan to a cooling rack set in the refrigerator to cool the top of the brownie slab before covering it with the roasted banana cream cheese frosting. Maintain the oven temperature at 350°F.

6   Line a quarter-sheet pan with aluminum foil. Place the unpeeled banana on the prepared baking pan. Using a cake tester (or toothpick) poke holes all over the top of the banana so it doesn't burst while in the oven. Roast until the skin turns black and clear liquid just starts to come out of the poked holes, about 15 minutes. Transfer the pan to the refrigerator for at least 30 minutes to cool down the roasted banana.

7   To make the roasted banana cream cheese frosting, place the cream cheese, butter, and salt in the small mixing bowl. Using a hand mixer on high speed, beat the mixture until it is light and fluffy. Peel the roasted banana and add it and the vanilla; beat until well combined. Add the confectioners' sugar to the bowl (no need to sift) and beat until creamy and smooth. Dollop the frosting over the cooled brownie slab and spread evenly with a small offset spatula. Place the pan in the freezer for 10 minutes to slightly firm up the frosting before preparing the chocolate glaze.

8   To make the chocolate glaze, slice the butter into ¼-inch thick slices. Place the butter slices and corn syrup in the reserved small saucepan and melt over the lowest setting. Meanwhile, place the bittersweet chocolate chips in a 2-cup Pyrex measuring cup. Microwave the chips on high power for 90 seconds, whisk with the reserved small whisk, then microwave an additional 15 seconds: whisk again. Pour the melted butter mixture into the melted chocolate and whisk gently until combined and completely smooth. Pour the glaze over the roasted banana cream cheese frosting and spread it evenly with a small offset spatula.

9   To make the garnish, using a nut chopper or chef's knife, finely chop the banana chips. If using a nut chopper, pour the mixture into a small bowl and repeat the process through the nut chopper 2 more times. Sprinkle the finely ground banana chips evenly over the warm chocolate glaze.

10 Refrigerate the pan for 7 to 8 hours, or overnight. See page xii for instructions on removing and cutting the slab, and for refrigerated storage (up to 5 days) and freezing guidelines.

Bananarama
Brownies

Crystallized Ginger
Brownies

holiday peppermint bark brownies

makes 12 large squares or 24 smaller bars

When you are an avid cook or baker, you get to know the folks who work at your local Williams-Sonoma store, and they get to know you. I wanted to create a brownie to pay homage to their famous Peppermint Bark, which goes flying out the door as soon as it appears in the stores.

brownie batter

Vegetable shortening for pan
2 (5.4-ounce) packages *peppermint bark squares
  (Ghirardelli)
2½ sticks (10 ounces) unsalted butter
¾ cup (4 ounces) 100% cacao unsweetened
  chocolate chips
1¼ cups (7.5 ounces) 63% extra dark
  chocolate chips
5 large eggs, at room temperature
1¼ cups (8.7 ounces) granulated sugar
1¼ packed cups (10 ounces) light brown sugar
1 teaspoon salt
2 teaspoons pure vanilla extract
1¼ cups (5.6 ounces) unbleached all-purpose flour
½ teaspoon and 1/8 teaspoon baking powder
*I prefer the dark chocolate peppermint bark squares

peppermint candy cane garnish

8 regular (4 ounces) peppermint candy canes (Brach's)

creamy white ganache

¾ cup (6 ounces) heavy whipping cream
3 cups (18 ounces) *Ghirardelli CLASSIC WHITE Premium
  Baking Chips
*I chose these chips because they have a whiter finish.

optional garnish

Candy cane icing decorations (Wilton)

1 Unwrap the peppermint bark squares and cut into ¼ to ½-inch dice. Set aside.

2 Adjust an oven rack to the middle level of the oven and preheat to 350°F. Prepare a 9 by 13-inch baking pan with heavy-duty aluminum foil as shown on page ix. Lightly grease the foil in the pan.

3 To make the brownie batter, cut the butter sticks into ½-inch slices. In a small, heavy saucepan, begin to melt the butter pieces over the lowest setting; add the unsweetened and extra dark chocolate chips. Stir with a small whisk until combined and the chocolate is melted and smooth. Turn off the heat, but leave the saucepan on the burner while proceeding with the recipe.

4 Using a large whisk, lightly beat the eggs in a large mixing bowl. Place the sugars and salt in a separate small mixing bowl, then whisk into the eggs just until incorporated. Briefly whisk the melted chocolate mixture, then gradually whisk into the egg mixture until just combined. Briefly whisk in the vanilla.

5 Place the flour and baking powder in the small mixing bowl; whisk together to combine. Sift through a medium strainer directly onto the batter; stir in with a silicone spatula until just combined. Pour half (1 pound 10 ounces) of the brownie batter into prepared pan. The best way to do this is ight. Place the prepared pan on a scale, t subtract) the weight of the pan, and scrape t rrect weight of batter directly into the pan. Spread the batter evenly with a small offset spatula.

6 Sprinkle the chopped peppermint bark over the batter. Dollop the remaining brownie batter evenly over the bark and carefully spread to the edges with the offset spatula, covering the bark. Bake for 34 minutes, until a toothpick inserted in the center of the slab comes out clean. Transfer the pan to a cooling rack. Note: While the brownie slab is baking, prepare the peppermint candy cane garnish.

7 To make the peppermint candy cane garnish, use your fingers to break the candy canes into approixmate 1 to 2-inch long pieces. Spread out a large sheet of parchment paper and place the candy cane pieces in a single layer on one side. Fold the parchment over the canes to cover, then fold up the edges of the paper so the candy is enclosed in the paper. Using a rolling pin, bang on the candy canes to crush the candy canes well, but not turn them entirely into dust. Pour the crus d candy canes into a small bowl and set aside.

8 To make the creamy te ganache, bring the cream just to a simmer er medium-high heat in a 2-quart saucier or sa pan. Remove the pan from the heat and add t white baking chips; shake the pan to cover chips with the hot cream. Return the pan to ourner (with the heat turned off) and blend gether with a small silicone spatula or whisk just until the chips are incorporated and completely melted. Pour the ganache over the warm brownie slab and spread evenly with a small offset spatula.

9 Sprinkle the crushed candy canes (and dust) over the warm ganache, then use the back of a metal spatula to lightly tap on the candy to slightly imbed it into the ganache. Refrigerate the pan for 7 to 8 hours, or overnight. See page xii for instructions on removing and cutting the slab, and for refrigerated storage (up to 2 weeks) and freezing guidelines.

*If desired: top each brownie with a Wilton Candy Cane Icing Decoration

Holiday Peppermint
Bark Brownies

campfire s'more brownies

makes 12 large squares or 24 smaller bars

This is a big, ooey, gooey brownie that I like to make for the 4th of July. If you don't have Golden Grahams cereal, feel free to break up graham crackers to use in the bark. Toasting the marshmallows under a broiler is a must to give the marshmallows that true "campfire" toasty flavor.

golden grahams bark
Vegetable shortening for pan
1 tablespoon (0.05 ounce) canola oil
1 cup (6 ounces) 60% cacao bittersweet chocolate chips
1½ cups (2 ounces) Golden Grahams cereal

milk chocolate brownie batter
Vegetable shortening for pan
2 sticks (8 ounces) unsalted butter
2²/₃ cups (1 pound) milk chocolate chips
4 large eggs, at room temperature
½ cup (3.5 ounces) granulated sugar
1 packed cup (8 ounces) light brown sugar
1 teaspoon salt
1 teaspoon pure vanilla extract
1½ cups (6.8 ounces) unbleached all-purpose flour
½ teaspoon baking powder
2 tablespoons Dutch-processed unsweetened
    cocoa powder
88 regular size marshmallows (Kraft Jet-Puffed) from 2
    (12-ounce) bags

1   To make the Golden Grahams bark, cut out a sheet of parchment paper to line the bottom of a quarter sheet pan. Lightly grease the bottom of the pan and place the parchment paper on top; press down to secure the paper onto the pan. Set aside.

2   Bring a medium saucepan with two inches of water just to a boil. Place the canola oil and bittersweet chocolate chips in a metal mixing bowl that will fit over the saucepan to form a double boiler. When the water comes to a boil, take the saucepan off the heat and place the mixing bowl over the hot water: the bottom of the metal bowl should not touch the hot water. Stir with a small silicone spatula until the chocolate is melted and perfectly smooth. Stir in the cereal. Remove the mixing bowl from the saucepan and using a kitchen towel, wipe off any condensation from the bottom of the mixing bowl. Scrape the mixture onto the parchment-lined pan. Using a small offset spatula, spread the mixture out evenly to about a ¼-inch height; the mixture should cover the parchment-lined pan with about an inch of free space around all the edges of the bark. Refrigerate the pan while proceeding with the recipe.

3   Adjust an oven rack to the middle level of the oven and preheat to 350°F. Prepare a 9 by 13-inch baking pan with heavy-duty aluminum foil as shown on page ix. Lightly grease the foil in the pan.

4   To make the milk chocolate brownie batter, cut the butter sticks into ½-inch slices. In a small, heavy saucepan, begin to melt the butter pieces over the lowest setting; add the milk chocolate chips. Stir with a small whisk until combined and the chocolate is melted and smooth. Turn off the heat. but leave the saucepan on the burner while proceeding with the recipe.

5   Using a large whisk, lightly beat the eggs in a large mixing bowl. Place the sugars and salt in a separate small mixing bowl, then whisk into the eggs just until incorporated. Briefly whisk the melted chocolate mixture, then gradually whisk into the egg mixture until just combined. Briefly whisk in the vanilla.

6   Place the flour, baking powder, and cocoa powder in the small mixing bowl; whisk together to combine. Sift through a medium strainer directly onto the batter; stir in with a silicone spatula until just combined. Pour the batter into the prepared pan and spread evenly with a small offset spatula. Bake for 34 minutes, until a toothpick inserted in the center of the slab comes out clean.

7   Remove the pan from the oven and place the marshmallows in a single layer in 11 rows of 8 marshmallows each, starting at one short end of the pan. The marshmallows should be tightly packed together. Return the pan to the oven and bake an additional 4 minutes, just until the marshmallows are nicely puffed but not browned. Transfer the pan to a cooling rack.

8   Set a rack in the upper third of the oven and set the oven to the Broil setting. Place the brownie pan back in the oven to lightly brown/toast the tops of the marshmallows, about 1 minute: WARNING: KEEP A CLOSE EYE ON THE MARSHMALLOWS TO MAKE SURE THEY DON'T OVERBROWN OR CATCH FIRE. Place the pan in the refrigerator for 10 minutes to cool down the marshmallow layer. Note: Chop the Golden Grahams bark while the marshmallow layer is cooling.

9   Using the parchment paper, transfer the chilled bark to a cutting board. Using a large chef's knife, coarsely chop the bark into approixmate ¼-inch dice. Sprinkle the chopped bark evenly over the marshmallow layer, then using the back of a metal spatula, lightly tap on the bark to slightly imbed it into the marshmallows. Refrigerate the pan for 7 to 8 hours, or overnight. See page xii for instructions on removing and cutting the slab, and for refrigerated storage (up to 2 weeks) and freezing guidelines.

note

Use kitchen shears to tidy up any ragged marshmallow edges after pulling off the aluminum foil from the slab.

Campfire S'more
Brownies

hazelnut nutella marshmallow brownies

makes 12 large squares or 24 smaller bars

Sometimes I taste one of my creations and I know I've nailed it, that is to say, to my own personal taste and satisfaction. This is a brownie I make often to be devoured exclusively by me over the course of a week or two. I'll just say it: this is probably my favorite brownie!

---

brownie batter
Vegetable shortening for pan
1 cup (4.5 ounces) skinned and roasted whole
    hazelnuts (Nature's Garden)
2 sticks (8 ounces) unsalted butter
1⅓ cups (8 ounces) 63% extra dark chocolate chips
4 large eggs, at room temperature
2 cups (14 ounces) sugar
¾ teaspoon salt
1½ teaspoons pure vanilla extract
¾ cup and 1 tablespoon (3.3 ounces) cake flour
¾ cup and 2 tablespoons (2.8 ounces) Dutch-processed
    unsweetened cocoa powder

hazelnut marshmallow
¾ cup (6 ounces) cold bottled spring water, divided
1 tablespoon and ¾ teaspoon unflavored gelatin (Knox)
1½ cups (10 ounces) sugar
½ teaspoon salt
½ cup (6 ounces) light corn syrup
2 teaspoons pure vanilla extract
1 teaspoon hazelnut flavoring (Cook's)

garnish
½ cup (5.5 ounces) chocolate hazelnut spread (Nutella)

1   Adjust an oven rack to the middle level of the oven
    and preheat to 350°F. Prepare a 9 by 13-inch baking
    pan with heavy-duty aluminum foil as shown on page
    ix. Lightly grease the foil in the pan.

2   Using a nut chopper or chef's knife, finely chop the
    hazelnuts. Set aside.

3   To make the brownie batter, cut the butter sticks into
    ½-inch slices. In a small, heavy saucepan, begin to
    melt the butter pieces over the lowest setting; add
    the extra dark chocolate chips. Stir with a small whisk
    until combined and the chocolate is melted and
    smooth. Turn off the heat, but leave the saucepan on
    the burner while proceeding with the recipe.

4   Using a large whisk, lightly beat the eggs in a large mixing bowl. Place the sugar and salt in a separate small mixing bowl, then whisk into the eggs just until incorporated. Briefly whisk the melted chocolate mixture, then gradually whisk into the egg mixture until just combined. Briefly whisk in the vanilla.

5   Place the flour and cocoa powder in the small mixing bowl; whisk together to combine. Sift through a medium strainer directly onto the batter; stir in with a silicone spatula until just combined. Sprinkle the chopped hazelnuts over the batter and fold in until just combined. Pour the batter into the prepared pan and spread evenly with a small offset spatula. Bake for 28 minutes, until a toothpick inserted in the center of the slab comes out clean. Transfer the pan to a cooling rack set in the refrigerator.

6   To make the hazelnut marshmallow, place ¼ cup and 2 tablespoons (3 ounces) of the water in the bowl of a stand mixer fitted with the paddle attachment. Sprinkle the gelatin over the surface of the water; set aside. Sift (or strain) the sugar into a 1½ to 2 quart heavy saucepan. Add the salt, corn syrup and remaining water. Place over medium-high heat and bring the mixture to a boil, stirring occasionally with a silicone spatula. Reduce the heat to the lowest setting, cover the pan, and boil for 2 minutes to allow any sugar crystals on the sides of the saucepan to dissolve. Remove the pan lid and increase the heat to medium-high. Insert a candy thermometer into the mixture and let the syrup boil without stirring until the temperature reaches 240°F.

7   With the mixer on the lowest speed, very gradually pour the syrup into the gelatin mixture. After all of the syrup has been added, increase the speed to high and beat for 12 minutes. Note: In the last 5 minutes of beating the marshmallow mixture, place the Nutella in a 1-cup Pyrex measuring cup and microwave on 50% power in 30 second intervals, just until the Nutella is warm and softened. Be careful not to over-microwave the Nutella; it can scorch like chocolate. Stir the Nutella with a teaspoon and set aside.

8   After the marshmallow mixture has beaten for 12 minutes, reduce the mixer speed to low and add the vanilla and hazelnut flavoring; mix until just incorporated, about 15 seconds. Increase the mixer speed to high and beat an additional minute. Use a pastry scraper to dollop the slightly warm and thick marshmallow over the top of the brownie slab; quickly smooth the top with a small offset spatula. Use the teaspoon to spoon the warmed Nutella into approixmate 1-inch spots randomly over the top of the marshmallow layer, then lightly swirl the mixtures together with the tip of the offset spatula to form a marbled pattern. Refrigerate the pan for 7 to 8 hours, or overnight. See page xii for instructions on removing and cutting the slab, and for refrigerated storage (up to 2 weeks) and freezing guidelines.

Hazelnut Nutella
Marshmallow Brownies

fudge marble
marshmallow brownies

makes 12 large squares or 24 smaller bars

I love chocolate covered marshmallow candies, like the egg-shaped ones available during the Easter season. However, I only like the dark chocolate covered eggs, which are harder to find than the milk chocolate covered eggs. This brownie satisfies my dark chocolate and marshmallow cravings all year round.

brownie batter

Vegetable shortening for pan
1½ sticks (6 ounces) unsalted butter
1 cup (6 ounces) 63% extra dark chocolate chips
3 large eggs, at room temperature
1½ cups (10.5 ounces) sugar
½ teaspoon salt
1 teaspoon pure vanilla extract
½ cup and 1½ tablespoons (2.5 ounces) cake flour
½ cup and 1 tablespoon (2.1 ounces) Dutch-processed
   unsweetened cocoa powder

vanilla marshmallow

1 cup (8 ounces) cold bottled spring water, divided
2 tablespoons and 1½ teaspoons unflavored
   gelatin (Knox)
2 cups (14 ounces) sugar
½ teaspoon salt
²/₃ cup (8 ounces) light corn syrup
2½ teaspoons pure vanilla extract
1 teaspoon clear vanilla extract

fudge sauce

¹/₃ cup (2 ounces) 63% extra dark chocolate chips
1 teaspoon (0.01 ounce) unsalted butter
4 teaspoons (0.03 ounce) Dutch-processed unsweetened
   cocoa powder
5 teaspoons (0.06 ounce) sugar
¼ cup (2 ounces) heavy whipping cream
¼ teaspoon pure vanilla extract

1   Adjust an oven rack to the middle level of the oven and preheat to 350°F. Prepare a 9 by 13-inch baking pan with heavy-duty aluminum foil as shown on page ix. Lightly grease the foil in the pan.

2   To make the brownie batter, cut the butter sticks into ½-inch slices. In a small, heavy saucepan, begin to melt the butter pieces over the lowest setting; add the extra dark chocolate chips. Stir with a small whisk until combined and the chocolate is melted and smooth. Turn off the heat, but leave the saucepan on the burner while proceeding with the recipe.

3   Using a large whisk, lightly beat the eggs in a large mixing bowl. Place the sugar and salt in a separate small mixing bowl, then whisk into the eggs just until incorporated. Briefly whisk the melted chocolate mixture, then gradually whisk into the egg mixture until just combined. Briefly whisk in the vanilla. Note: Set aside the saucepan and small whisk (no need to wash them) to use later for the fudge sauce.

4   Place the flour and cocoa powder in the small mixing bowl; whisk together to combine. Sift through a medium strainer directly onto the batter; stir in with a silicone spatula until just combined. Pour the batter into the prepared pan and spread evenly with a small offset spatula. Bake for 23 minutes, until a toothpick inserted in the center of the slab comes out clean. Transfer the pan to a cooling rack set in the refrigerator.

5   To make the vanilla marshmallow, place ½ cup (4 ounces) of the water in the bowl of a stand mixer fitted with the paddle attachment. Sprinkle the gelatin over the surface of the water; set aside. Sift (or strain) the sugar into a 1½ to 2 quart heavy saucepan. Add the salt, corn syrup and remaining water. Place over medium-high heat and bring the mixture to a boil, stirring occasionally with a silicone spatula. Reduce the heat to the lowest setting, cover the pan, and boil for 2 minutes to allow any sugar crystals on the sides of the saucepan to dissolve. Remove the pan lid and increase the heat to medium-high. Insert a candy thermometer into the mixture and let the syrup boil without stirring until the temperature reaches 240°F.

6   With the mixer on the lowest speed, very gradually pour the syrup into the gelatin mixture. After all of the syrup has been added, very gradually (so the hot syrup does not splash up out of the mixing bowl) increase the speed to high and beat for 15 minutes. Note: While the marshmallow is beating, prepare the fudge sauce.

7   To make the fudge sauce, place the chocolate chips in a small bowl. Cut the butter into tiny 1/8-inch dice. Set aside.

8   Sift the cocoa powder through a medium strainer directly into the reserved saucepan (or 1-quart saucier.) Add the sugar and cream to the pan and whisk together using the small whisk. Bring the mixture just to a simmer over medium-high heat, whisking constantly. Remove the pan from the heat and whisk in the chocolate chips and butter bits until smooth. Whisk in the vanilla. Set aside at room temperature.

9   After the marshmallow mixture has beaten for 15 minutes, reduce the mixer speed to low and add the vanilla extracts; mix until just incorporated, about 15 seconds. Increase the mixer speed to high and beat an additional minute. Use a pastry scraper to dollop the slightly warm and thick marshmallow over the top of the brownie slab; quickly smooth the top with a small offset spatula. Using a small silicone spatula, drizzle the warm fudge sauce randomly over the top of the marshmallow layer, then lightly swirl the mixtures together with the tip of the offset spatula to form a marbled pattern. Refrigerate the pan for 7 to 8 hours, or overnight. See page xii for instructions on removing and cutting the slab, and for refrigerated storage (up to 2 weeks) and freezing guidelines.

Fudge Marble
Marshmallow Brownies

crazy good caramel marshmallow brownies

makes 12 large squares or 24 smaller bars

After I created my Dulce de Leche Cheesecake Brownies, I started thinking about what to do with the rest of that wonderful dulce de leche besides drizzling it over ice cream. It became a key ingredient in a delicious caramel marshmallow. Hershey's Sea Salt Caramel chips are usually sold in grocery stores only during the holiday season, but you can buy them year round from the Hershey's website or on Amazon.

brownie batter
Vegetable shortening for pan
2½ sticks (10 ounces) unsalted butter
¾ cup (4 ounces) 100% cacao unsweetened chocolate chips
1¼ cups (7.5 ounces) 63% extra dark chocolate chips
5 large eggs, at room temperature
1¼ cups (8.7 ounces) granulated sugar
1¼ packed cups (10 ounces) light brown sugar
1 teaspoon salt
2 teaspoons pure vanilla extract
1¼ cups (5.6 ounces) unbleached all-purpose flour
½ teaspoon and 1/8 teaspoon baking powder
1 cup (6 ounces) sea salt caramel chips (Hershey's)

caramel marshmallow layer
¾ cup (6 ounces) cold bottled spring water, divided
2 tablespoons unflavored gelatin (Knox)
1½ cups (10.5 ounces) granulated sugar
½ teaspoon salt
½ cup and 1 tablespoon (6 ounces) light corn syrup
¼ cup (2.6 ounces) dulce de leche (Nestlé La Lechera)
2 teaspoons caramel flavor

garnish
2 tablespoons dark chocolate crispearls
2 tablespoons salted caramel crispearls

1 Adjust an oven rack to the middle level of the oven and preheat to 350°F. Prepare a 9 by 13-inch baking pan with heavy-duty aluminum foil as shown on page ix. Lightly grease the foil in the pan.

2 To make the brownie batter, cut the butter sticks into ½-inch slices. In a small, heavy saucepan, melt the butter pieces over the lowest setting; add the unsweetened and extra dark chocolate chips. Stir with a small whisk until combined and the chocolate is melted and smooth. Turn off the heat, but leave the saucepan on the burner while proceeding with the recipe.

3 Using a large whisk, lightly beat the eggs in a large mixing bowl. Place the sugars and salt in a separate small mixing bowl, then whisk into the eggs just until incorporated. Briefly whisk the melted chocolate mixture, then gradually whisk into the egg mixture until just combined. Briefly whisk in the vanilla.

4 Place the flour and baking powder in the small mixing bowl; whisk together to combine. Sift through a medium strainer directly onto the batter; stir in with a silicone spatula until just combined. Sprinkle the caramel chips over the batter and fold in until just combined. Pour the batter into the prepared pan and spread evenly with a small offset spatula. Bake for 34 minutes, until a toothpick inserted in the center of the slab comes out clean. Transfer the pan to a cooling rack set in the refrigerator.

5 To make the caramel marshmallow layer, place ¼ cup and 2 tablespoons (3 ounces) of the water in the bowl of a stand mixer fitted with the paddle attachment. Sprinkle the gelatin over the surface of the water; set aside. Sift (or strain) the sugar into a 1½ to 2 quart heavy saucepan. Add the salt, corn syrup and remaining water. Place over medium-high heat and bring the mixture to a boil, stirring occasionally with a silicone spatula. Reduce the heat to the lowest setting, cover the pan, and boil for 2 minutes to allow any sugar crystals on the sides of the saucepan to dissolve. Remove the pan lid and increase the heat to medium-high. Insert a candy thermometer into the mixture, and let the syrup boil without stirring until the temperature reaches 240°F.

6 With the mixer on the lowest speed, gradually pour the syrup into the gelatin mixture. After all of the syrup has been added, very gradually (so the hot syrup does not splash up out of the mixing bowl) increase the speed to high and beat for 12 minutes.

7 After the marshmallow mixture has beaten for 12 minutes, reduce the mixer speed to low and add the dulce de leche and the caramel flavor; mix until just incorporated, about 15 seconds. Increase the mixer speed to high and beat an additional minute. Use a pastry scraper to dollop the slightly warm and thick marshmallow over the top of the brownie slab; quickly smooth the top with a small offset spatula. Immediately garnish with the crispearls, sprinkled randomly over the marshmallow. Refrigerate the pan for 7 to 8 hours, or overnight. See page xii for instructions on removing and cutting the slab, and for refrigerated storage (up to 2 weeks) and freezing guidelines.

Crazy Good Caramel
Marshmallow Brownies

strawberry fields marshmallow brownies

makes 12 large squares or 24 smaller bars

When strawberries are ripe in the fields, I go picking! As soon as I get home I rinse the berries with cold water and gently pat them dry with paper towels. I stem and cut them in half, then weigh them out into 8-ounce portions (to use in recipes like this) into FoodSaver® bags with the tops still open, which I place standing upright on a sheet pan in the freezer. When the berry halves are frozen, I pulse out as much air as possible and vacuum-seal the tops of the bags with the FoodSaver® machine. Freezing does make some of the juices come out when thawed, so if you are using fresh strawberries you may not have strawberry juice; just substitute water for the strawberry juice used in the jam.

strawberry jam
1½ cups (8 ounces) frozen (or fresh) strawberry halves
⅓ cup and 2 tablespoons (3.1 ounces) sugar
2 tablespoons and 2 teaspoons cornstarch
3 tablespoons (reserved strawberry juice) from thawed strawberries
Optional: 1 to 2 teaspoons fresh lemon juice

brownie batter
Vegetable shortening for pan
2 sticks (8 ounces) unsalted butter
½ cup and 1 tablespoon (3 ounces) 100% cacao unsweetened chocolate chips
1 cup (6 ounces) 63% extra dark chocolate chips
4 large eggs, at room temperature
1 cup (7 ounces) granulated sugar
1 packed cup (8 ounces) light brown sugar
¾ teaspoon salt

1½ teaspoons pure vanilla extract
1 cup (4.5 ounces) unbleached all-purpose flour
½ teaspoon baking powder

strawberry marshmallow
¾ cup (6 ounces) cold bottled spring water, divided
2 tablespoons unflavored gelatin (Knox)
1½ cups (10.5 ounces) sugar
½ teaspoon salt
½ cup (6 ounces) light corn syrup
½ cup (4 ounces) strawberry jam (from above recipe)
2 teaspoons pure strawberry extract

garnish
strawberry jam (from above recipe)

1   To make the strawberry jam, thaw the strawberries overnight in the refrigerator. Drain the strawberries in a sieve set over a bowl to collect and reserve the strawberry juice. Using the finest disc of a food mill set over a mixing bowl, puree the strawberries. Note: Alternately, use a blender or food processor to puree the strawberries.

2   Combine the pureed strawberries, sugar, cornstarch, and strawberry juice in a 1-quart saucier (or saucepan) with a small whisk. Cook over medium-high heat, whisking occasionally, until the mixture thickens and comes to a boil. Boil for 30 seconds, whisking constantly. Remove the pan from the heat and taste the jam: if you feel it is too sweet (it depends on the ripeness of your strawberries) whisk in 1 to 2 teaspoons fresh lemon juice. Transfer the jam to a 2-cup Pyrex measuring cup: there should be a little over 1 cup. Keep the jam at room temperature (uncovered) while proceeding with the recipe.

3   Adjust an oven rack to the middle level of the oven and preheat to 350°F.

4   Cut out a sheet of parchment paper to measure 9½ x 13½ inches. Lightly grease the bottom and interior sides of a 9 by 13-inch baking pan with a *removable bottom. Place the parchment paper on the bottom of the pan to come ¼-inch up the sides of the pan. Lightly grease the parchment paper. Set aside. *Note: If you don't have a pan with a removable bottom, prepare a regular 9 by 13-inch pan with foil as directed on page ix.

5   To make the brownie batter, cut the butter sticks into ½-inch slices. In a small, heavy saucepan, melt the butter pieces over the lowest setting; add the unsweetened and extra dark chocolate chips. Stir with a small whisk until combined and the chocolate is melted and smooth. Turn off the heat, but leave the saucepan on the burner while proceeding with the recipe.

6   Using a large whisk, lightly beat the eggs in a large mixing bowl. Place the sugars and salt in a separate small mixing bowl, then whisk into the eggs just until incorporated. Briefly whisk the melted chocolate mixture, then gradually whisk into the egg mixture until just combined. Briefly whisk in the vanilla.

7   Place the flour and baking powder in the small mixing bowl; whisk together to combine. Sift through a medium strainer directly onto the batter; stir in with a silicone spatula until just combined. Pour the batter into the prepared pan and spread evenly with a small offset spatula. Bake for 28 minutes, until a toothpick inserted in the center of the slab comes out clean. Transfer the pan to a cooling rack set in the refrigerator.

8   To make the strawberry marshmallow, place ¼ cup and 2 tablespoons (3 ounces) of the water in the bowl of a stand mixer fitted with the whisk attachment. Sprinkle the gelatin over the surface of the water; set aside. Sift (or strain) the sugar into a 1½ to 2 quart heavy saucepan. Add the salt, corn syrup and remaining water. Place over medium-high heat and bring the mixture to a boil, stirring occasionally with a silicone spatula. Reduce the heat to the lowest setting, cover the pan, and boil for 2 minutes to allow any sugar crystals on the sides of the saucepan to dissolve. Remove the pan lid and increase the heat to medium-high. Insert a candy thermometer into the mixture and let the syrup boil without stirring until the temperature reaches 240°F.

9   With the mixer on the lowest speed, gradually pour the syrup into the gelatin mixture. After all of the syrup has been added, very gradually (so the hot syrup does not splash up out of the mixing bowl) increase the speed to high and beat for 12 minutes.

10 After the marshmallow mixture has beaten for 12 minutes, reduce the mixer speed to low and add ½ cup (4 ounces) of the strawberry jam and the strawberry extract and mix until incorporated, about 15 seconds. Increase the mixer speed to high and beat an additional minute. Use a pastry scraper to dollop the slightly warm and thick marshmallow over the top of the brownie slab; quickly smooth the top with a small offset spatula.

11 Use a teaspoon to dollop the remaining strawberry jam into approixmate ½ to 1-inch spots randomly over the top of the marshmallow layer, then lightly swirl the mixtures together with the tip of the small offset spatula to form a marbled pattern. Refrigerate the pan for 7 to 8 hours, or overnight.

12 To remove the brownie slab from the pan, run a thin knife between the slab and the sides of the pan. Push the bottom of the pan up out of the sides and place it on a cutting board. Use a long chef's knife to cut it into 12 large squares, cleaning the knife in hot water and drying before each cut to provide sharp clean edges. See page xiv for refrigerated storage (up to 1 week) and freezing guidelines.

"Strawberry Fields"
Marshmallow Brownies

after midnight candy bar brownies

makes 12 large squares or 24 smaller bars

I have found over the years that many American candy bars coated in chocolate have lost their true "chocolate" flavor, so when given the choice, I always opt for the dark chocolate version of a candy bar to get more of a chocolate punch. To continue the candy bar theme, I incorporated white chocolate nougat and crispy candy "pearls" onto this fantastic brownie.

brownie batter

Vegetable shortening for pan
40 Midnight Milky Way minis from 2 (8.90-ounce) packages
2 sticks (8 ounces) unsalted butter
1⅓ cups (8 ounces) 63% extra dark chocolate chips
4 large eggs, at room temperature
2 cups (14 ounces) sugar
¾ teaspoon salt
1½ teaspoons pure vanilla extract
¾ cup and 1 tablespoon (3.3 ounces) cake flour
¾ cup and 2 tablespoons (2.8 ounces) Dutch-processed unsweetened cocoa powder

white chip nougat

2¼ cups (10.8 ounces) marshmallow fluff or crème
1⅓ cups (8 ounces) white baking chips (Guittard Choc-Au-Lait)
6 tablespoons (3 ounces) unsalted butter
1½ cups (10.5 ounces) granulated sugar
⅓ cup and 1 teaspoon (3.3 ounces) evaporated milk
½ teaspoon salt
2 teaspoons pure vanilla extract

chocolate glaze

6 tablespoons (3 ounces) unsalted butter
1 tablespoon (0.08 ounce) light corn syrup
1 cup (6 ounces) 60% cacao bittersweet chocolate chips

garnish

3 tablespoons white chocolate Crispearls (Callebaut)

1   Adjust an oven rack to the middle level of the oven and preheat to 350°F. Prepare a 9 by 13-inch baking pan with heavy-duty aluminum foil as shown on page ix. Lightly grease the foil in the pan.

2   Unwrap the candy bars and place in a small bowl; set aside.

3   To make the brownie batter, cut the butter sticks into ½-inch slices. In a small, heavy saucepan, begin to melt the butter pieces over the lowest setting; add the extra dark chocolate chips. Stir with a small whisk until combined and the chocolate is melted and smooth. Turn off the heat, but leave the saucepan on the burner while proceeding with the recipe.

4   Using a large whisk, lightly beat the eggs in a large mixing bowl. Place the sugar and salt in a separate small mixing bowl, then whisk into the eggs just until incorporated. Briefly whisk the melted chocolate mixture, then gradually whisk into the egg mixture until just combined. Briefly whisk in the vanilla. Note: Set aside the saucepan (no need to wash it) to use later for the chocolate drizzle.

5   Place the flour and cocoa powder in the small mixing bowl; whisk together to combine. Sift through a medium strainer directly onto the batter; stir in with a silicone spatula until just combined. Pour the batter into the prepared pan and spread evenly with a small offset spatula. Push the candy bars into the batter in eight rows of five bars each: do not place any within 1-inch of the pan sides. Use the offset spatula to cover the candy with the batter. Bake for 32 minutes, until a toothpick inserted in the center of the slab comes out clean. Transfer the pan to a cooling rack set in the refrigerator.

6   To make the white chip nougat, place the marshmallow fluff in a bowl; set aside. Place the white chips in a separate small bowl; set aside.

7   Cut the butter into ¼-inch slices. Place the butter, sugar, and evaporated milk in a medium (2-quart) saucepan. Cook over medium-low heat, stirring occasionally with a silicone spatula, until the butter is melted and the sugar is dissolved. Increase the heat to medium-high and bring the mixture to a boil, then reduce the heat to the lowest setting and boil for 5 minutes, occasionally stirring the mixture to prevent the bottom from scorching. Remove the pan from the heat and stir in the salt, fluff and white chips, stirring vigorously until the mixture is well blended and the white chips are melted and smooth. Stir in the vanilla. Pour the nougat over the brownie slab and spread evenly with a small offset spatula. Refrigerate the pan while preparing the chocolate glaze.

8   To make the chocolate glaze, slice the butter into ¼-inch slices. Place the butter slices and corn syrup in the reserved small saucepan and melt over the lowest setting. Meanwhile, place the chocolate chips in a 2-cup Pyrex measuring cup. Microwave the chips on high power for 90 seconds, whisk with the reserved small whisk, then microwave an additional 15 seconds: whisk again. Pour the melted butter mixture into the melted chocolate and whisk gently until combined and completely smooth. Pour the glaze over the chocolate nougat layer and spread evenly with a small offset spatula. Transfer the pan to the refrigerator for 20 minutes to cool the glaze, then sprinkle the white chocolate crispearls over the glaze. Refrigerate the pan for 7 to 8 hours, or overnight. See page xii for instructions on removing and cutting the slab, and for refrigerated storage (up to 2 weeks) and freezing guidelines.

After Midnight
Candy Bar Brownies

3 musketeers chocolate nougat brownies

makes 12 large squares or 24 smaller bars

Let me point out the obvious: yes, these brownies are very similar to my After Midnight Candy Bar Brownies. Here's the thing: I REALLY like them both, so each recipe made the cut. I think it would be fun someday to make them both, cut them into bars, and present them on a dessert platter together and let folks decide which they like best.

brownie batter

Vegetable shortening for pan
20 Fun Size 3 Musketeers candy bars from 1 (10.48-ounce) package
2 sticks (8 ounces) unsalted butter
½ cup and 1 tablespoon (3 ounces) 100% cacao unsweetened chocolate chips
1 cup (6 ounces) 63% extra dark chocolate chips
4 large eggs, at room temperature
1 cup (7 ounces) granulated sugar
1 packed cup (8 ounces) light brown sugar
¾ teaspoon salt
1½ teaspoons pure vanilla extract
1 cup (4.5 ounces) unbleached all-purpose flour
½ teaspoon baking powder

chocolate nougat

2¼ cups (10.8 ounces) marshmallow fluff or crème
1 cup (6 ounces) 60% cacao bittersweet chocolate chips
6 tablespoons (3 ounces) unsalted butter
1½ cups (10.5 ounces) granulated sugar
$1/3$ cup and 1 teaspoon (3.3 ounces) evaporated milk
½ teaspoon salt
1 teaspoon pure vanilla extract
1 teaspoon pure chocolate extract

chocolate glaze

6 tablespoons (3 ounces) unsalted butter
1 tablespoon (0.08 ounce) light corn syrup
1 cup (6 ounces) 60% cacao bittersweet chocolate chips

garnish

4 tablespoons milk chocolate crispearls

1. Adjust an oven rack to the middle level of the oven and preheat to 350°F. Prepare a 9 by 13-inch baking pan with heavy-duty aluminum foil as shown on page ix. Lightly grease the foil in the pan.

2. Unwrap the candy bars and place in a small bowl; set aside.

3. To make the brownie batter, cut the butter sticks into ½-inch slices. In a small, heavy saucepan, melt the butter pieces over the lowest setting; add the unsweetened and extra dark chocolate chips. Stir with a small whisk until combined and the chocolate is melted and smooth. Turn off the heat, but leave the saucepan on the burner while proceeding with the recipe.

4. Using a large whisk, lightly beat the eggs in a large mixing bowl. Place the sugars and salt in a separate small mixing bowl, then whisk into the eggs just until incorporated. Briefly whisk the melted chocolate mixture, then gradually whisk into the egg mixture until just combined. Briefly whisk in the vanilla. Note: Set aside the saucepan and small whisk (no need to wash them) to use later for the chocolate glaze.

5. Place the flour and baking powder in the small mixing bowl; whisk together to combine. Sift through a medium strainer directly onto the batter; stir in with a silicone spatula until just combined. Pour the batter into the prepared pan and spread evenly with a small offset spatula. Push the candy bars into the batter on the diagonal in five rows of four bars each: do not place any within ½-inch of the pan sides. Use the offset spatula to cover the candy with the batter. Bake for 30 minutes, until a toothpick inserted in the center of the slab comes out clean. Transfer the pan to a cooling rack set in the refrigerator.

6. To make the chocolate nougat, place the fluff in a medium bowl; set aside. Place the bittersweet chocolate chips in a separate small bowl; set aside.

7. Cut the butter into ¼-inch thick slices. Place the butter, sugar, and evaporated milk in a medium (2-quart) saucepan. Cook over medium-low heat, stirring occasionally with a silicone spatula, until the butter is melted and the sugar is dissolved. Increase the heat to medium-high and bring the mixture to a boil, then reduce the heat to the lowest setting and boil for 5 minutes, occasionally stirring the mixture to prevent the bottom from scorching. Remove the pan from the heat and stir in the salt, fluff and chocolate chips, stirring vigorously until the mixture is well blended and the chocolate chips are melted and smooth. Stir in the extracts. Pour the nougat over the brownie slab and spread evenly with a small offset spatula. Refrigerate the pan while preparing the chocolate glaze.

8. To make the chocolate glaze, slice the butter into ¼-inch slices. Place the butter slices and corn syrup in the reserved small saucepan and melt over the lowest setting. Meanwhile, place the chocolate chips in a 2-cup Pyrex measuring cup. Microwave the chips on high power for 90 seconds, whisk with the reserved small whisk, then microwave an additional 15 seconds: whisk again. Pour the melted butter mixture into the melted chocolate and whisk gently until combined and completely smooth. Pour the glaze over the chocolate nougat layer and spread evenly with a small offset spatula, then sprinkle the chocolate crispearls over the glaze. Refrigerate the pan for 7 to 8 hours, or overnight. See page xii for instructions on removing and cutting the slab, and for refrigerated storage (up to 2 weeks) and freezing guidelines.

3 Musketeers Chocolate
Nougat Brownies

mounds of joy brownies

makes 12 large squares or 24 smaller bars

I am as much a coconut freak as I am a chocolate freak, so combining the two makes me like, totally freak out. This decadent brownie has snack size Mounds bars baked inside, then covered with a layer of white chip nougat, toasted coconut flakes, and big chunks of almonds that can easily be removed, because sometimes you feel like a nut, and sometimes you don't!

brownie batter

Vegetable shortening for pan
20 snack size Mounds candy bars from two (11.3-ounce) packages
2 sticks (8 ounces) unsalted butter
1⅓ cups (8 ounces) 63% extra dark chocolate chips
4 large eggs, at room temperature
2 cups (14 ounces) sugar
1 teaspoon salt
1½ teaspoons pure vanilla extract
¾ cup and 1 tablespoon (3.3 ounces) cake flour
¾ cup and 2 tablespoons (2.8 ounces) Dutch-processed unsweetened cocoa powder

white chip nougat

1½ cups (7.2 ounces) marshmallow fluff or crème
²/₃ cup (4 ounces) white baking chips (Guittard Choc-AuLait)
4 tablespoons (2 ounces) unsalted butter
1 cup (7 ounces) sugar
¼ cup (2.2 ounces) evaporated milk
¼ teaspoon salt
¾ teaspoon pure vanilla extract

garnish

½ cup (1 ounce) organic unsweetened coconut flakes
¹/₃ cup (1.5 ounces) roasted salted whole almonds

chocolate drizzle

1½ teaspoons (0.03 ounce) unsalted butter
½ teaspoon (0.01 ounce) light corn syrup
1½ tablespoons (0.08 ounce) Special Dark chocolate chips (Hershey's)
1 teaspoon very hot water

1. Adjust an oven rack to the middle level of the oven and preheat to 350°F. Prepare a 9 by 13-inch baking pan with heavy-duty aluminum foil as shown on page ix. Lightly grease the foil in the pan.

2. Unwrap the candy bars and place in a small bowl; set aside.

3. To make the brownie batter, cut the butter sticks into ½-inch slices. In a small, heavy saucepan, begin to melt the butter pieces over the lowest setting; add the extra dark chocolate chips. Stir with a small whisk until combined and the chocolate is melted and smooth. Turn off the heat, but leave the saucepan on the burner while proceeding with the recipe.

4. Using a large whisk, lightly beat the eggs in a large mixing bowl. Place the sugar and salt in a separate small mixing bowl, then whisk into the eggs just until incorporated. Briefly whisk the melted chocolate mixture, then gradually whisk into the egg mixture until just combined. Briefly whisk in the vanilla. Note: Set aside the saucepan (no need to wash it) to use later for the chocolate drizzle.

5. Place the flour and cocoa powder in the small mixing bowl; whisk together to combine. Sift through a medium strainer directly onto the batter; stir in with a silicone spatula until just combined. Pour the batter into the prepared pan and spread evenly with a small offset spatula. Push the candy bars into the batter on the diagonal in five rows of four bars each: do not place any within ½-inch of the pan sides. Use the offset spatula to cover the candy with the batter. Bake for 30 minutes, until a toothpick inserted in the center of the slab comes out clean. Transfer the pan to a cooling rack set in the refrigerator. Note: while the oven is still at 350°F. toast the unsweetened coconut flakes for the garnish. Spread the coconut out evenly onto a quarter sheet pan. Toast for 3 to 4 minutes, until the coconut is fragrant and nicely browned. Transfer the pan to a cooling rack.

6. To make the white chip nougat, place the marshmallow fluff in a bowl; set aside. Place the white chips in a separate small bowl; set aside.

7. Cut the butter into ¼-inch slices. Place the butter, sugar, and evaporated milk in a medium (1½ to 2-quart) saucepan. Cook over medium-low heat, stirring occasionally with a silicone spatula, until the butter is melted and the sugar is dissolved. Increase the heat to medium-high and bring the mixture to a boil, then reduce the heat to the lowest setting and boil for 5 minutes, occasionally stirring the mixture to prevent the bottom from scorching. Remove the pan from the heat and stir in the salt, fluff and white chips, stirring vigorously until the mixture is well blended and the white chips are melted and smooth. Stir in the vanilla. Pour the nougat over the brownie slab and spread evenly with a small offset spatula. Immediately sprinkle the nougat with the toasted coconut. Cut the almonds in half widthwise, then place them randomly over the top of the nougat. Use the back of a metal spatula to lightly tap on the coconut and almonds to slightly imbed them into the nougat.

8. To make the chocolate drizzle, melt the butter and corn syrup over low heat in the reserved small saucepan. Remove the pan from the heat and add the chocolate chips; stir with a small silicone spatula until the chocolate is melted and smooth. Stir in the hot water to thin out. Using the spatula, drizzle thin, random "stripes" over the top of the brownie slab. Let the drizzle cool at room temperature for 30 minutes, then refrigerate the pan for 7 to 8 hours, or overnight. See page xii for instructions on removing and cutting the slab, and for refrigerated storage (up to 2 weeks) and freezing guidelines.

Mounds Of Joy
Brownies

radical reese's pieces brownies

I had experimented with placing chocolate M&M's in brownies before, but they just seemed to get lost without contributing much to the finished product. To my delight, I found that peanut butter flavored Reese's Pieces brought a lot to the "brownie party" and thus were a great addition. This brownie is like eating a terrific candy bar, only better. Listen to me: make this brownie!

chocolate peanut bark

Vegetable shortening for pan
¾ cup (3.5 ounces) salted peanuts (Virginia)
2 teaspoons (0.03 ounce) canola oil
¾ cup (4 ounces) 60% cacao bittersweet chocolate chips
¼ cup (1.8 ounces) *Reese's Pieces Minis Dessert Topping
*Found in the ice cream dessert topping section of grocery stores. If unavailable, randomly sprinkle regular-sized Reese's Pieces (from a 4-ounce box) along with the chopped bark over top of the peanut butter ganache: see Step #10.

brownie batter

Vegetable shortening for pan
2½ sticks (10 ounces) unsalted butter
¾ cup (4 ounces) 100% cacao unsweetened chocolate chips
1¼ cups (7.5 ounces) 63% extra dark chocolate chips
5 large eggs, at room temperature
1¼ cups (8.7 ounces) granulated sugar
1¼ packed cups (10 ounces) light brown sugar
1 teaspoon salt
2 teaspoons pure vanilla extract
1¼ cups (5.6 ounces) unbleached all-purpose flour

½ teaspoon and ⅛ teaspoon baking powder
1 (9.9-ounce) pouch Reese's Pieces

peanut butter ganache

⅔ cup and 1 tablespoon (5.5 ounces) heavy whipping cream
1 (10-ounce) package peanut butter baking chips (Reese's)

garnish

2 to 3 tablespoons Reese's Pieces Minis Dessert Topping

1   To make the chocolate peanut bark, cut out a sheet of parchment paper to line the bottom of a quarter sheet pan. Lightly grease the bottom of the pan and place the parchment paper on top; press down to secure the paper onto the pan. Set aside.

2   Using a nut chopper or chef's knife, finely chop the peanuts. Set aside.

3   Bring a medium saucepan with two inches of water just to a boil. Place the canola oil and chocolate chips

in a metal mixing bowl that will fit over the saucepan to form a double boiler. When the water comes to a boil, take the saucepan off the heat and place the mixing bowl over the hot water: the bottom of the metal bowl should not touch the hot water. Stir with a small silicone spatula until the chocolate is melted and perfectly smooth. Stir in the chopped peanuts. Remove the mixing bowl from the saucepan and using a kitchen towel, wipe off any condensation from the bottom of the mixing bowl. Scrape the mixture onto the parchment-lined pan. Using a small offset spatula, spread the chocolate evenly to about ¼-inch thickness. Sprinkle the mini Reese's Pieces evenly over the warm chocolate. Refrigerate the pan while proceeding with the recipe.

4   Adjust an oven rack to the middle level of the oven and preheat to 350°F. Prepare a 9 by 13-inch baking pan with heavy-duty aluminum foil as shown on page ix. Lightly grease the foil in the pan.

5   To make the brownie batter, cut the butter sticks into ½-inch slices. In a small, heavy saucepan, melt the butter pieces over the lowest setting; add the unsweetened and extra dark chocolate chips. Stir with a small whisk until combined and the chocolate is melted and smooth. Turn off the heat, but leave the saucepan on the burner while proceeding with the recipe.

6   Using a large whisk, lightly beat the eggs in a large mixing bowl. Place the sugars and salt in a separate small mixing bowl, then whisk into the eggs just until incorporated. Briefly whisk the melted chocolate mixture, then gradually whisk into the egg mixture until just combined. Briefly whisk in the vanilla. Note: Set aside the saucepan and small whisk (no need to wash them) to use later for the peanut butter ganache. The small amount of chocolate left in the pan and on the whisk is of no consequence when making the peanut butter ganache.

7   Place the flour and baking powder in the small mixing bowl; whisk together to combine. Sift through a medium strainer directly onto the batter; stir in with a silicone spatula until just combined. Sprinkle the Reese's Pieces over the batter and fold in until just combined. Pour the batter into the prepared pan and spread evenly with a small offset spatula. Bake for 34 minutes, until a toothpick inserted in the center of the slab comes out clean. Transfer the pan to a cooling rack.

8   To make the peanut butter ganache, bring the cream just to a simmer over medium-high heat in the reserved saucepan. Remove the pan from the heat and add the peanut butter chips; shake the pan to cover the chips with the hot cream. Cover the pan tightly and let sit off the heat for 2 minutes. Place the pan back on the burner (still turned off) and gently blend the cream and chips together with the small whisk just until the peanut butter chips are melted and smooth. Pour the ganache over the warm slab and spread evenly with a small offset spatula. Place the pan in the refrigerator for 20 minutes to cool down the ganache. Note: Chop the chocolate peanut bark while the ganache is cooling.

9   Using the parchment paper, transfer the chilled bark to a cutting board. Using a large chef's knife, coarsely chop the bark into approxixmate ¼-inch dice. Place the chopped bark in a small bowl and place in the freezer to chill while the ganache continues to cool in the refrigerator.

10 Sprinkle the chopped bark over the ganache. Sprinkle the mini (or regular) Reese's Pieces randomly over the chopped bark. Refrigerate the pan for 7 to 8 hours, or overnight. See page xii for instructions on removing and cutting the slab, and for refrigerated storage (up to 2 weeks) and freezing guidelines.

polka dot red velvet cheesecake brownies

makes 12 large squares or 24 smaller bars

It seemed natural to make a red velvet cheesecake brownie since cream cheese is traditionally a component of any "red velvet" dessert item. I wanted the cheesecake to be a part of (and not just on top of) the brownie itself, so I came up with the idea of injecting the cheesecake batter into the brownie batter using a pastry tip. The resulting "polka dots" of cheesecake end up being visible in the brownie as well as on top. Voila!

vanilla cheesecake batter

2 packages (8-ounces each) cream cheese, at
  room temperature
¼ teaspoon salt
²/₃ cup (4.7 ounces) sugar
1 large egg, at room temperature
2 teaspoons pure vanilla extract

brownie batter

Vegetable shortening for pan
2¼ sticks (10 ounces) unsalted butter
3¹/₃ cups (1 pound 4 ounces) milk chocolate chips
5 large eggs, at room temperature
½ cup and 2 tablespoons (4.4 ounces) granulated s
1¼ packed cups (10 ounces) light brown sugar
1 teaspoon salt
1 teaspoon chocolate extract
2 tablespoons (1 ounce) red food color
2 cups (9 ounces) unbleached all-purpose flour
1 teaspoon baking powder
3 tablespoons Dutch-processed unsweetened
  cocoa powder

1   Fit a medium (14-inch) pastry bag with a plain ¼-inch round pastry tip (Ateco #803). Set aside. Note: For this recipe, I use a large pastry bag coupler so that the pastry tip extends beyond the end of the pastry bag, but a pastry bag coupler is not required.

2   To make the vanilla cheesecake batter, cut the cream cheese into 1-inch slices and place in a small mixing bowl; add the salt. Using a hand mixer on high speed, beat until creamy. On medium speed, gradually add the sugar and beat an additional minute, scraping the bowl once to make sure the mixture is perfectly smooth. Add the egg and vanilla; beat until just combined. Scrape down the sides of the bowl and beat again briefly. Use a silicone spatula to dollop the cheesecake batter into the pastry bag. Set aside.

3   Adjust an oven rack to the middle level of the oven and preheat to 350°F. Prepare a 9 by 13-inch baking pan with heavy-duty aluminum foil as shown on page ix. Lightly grease the foil in the pan.

4   To make the brownie batter, cut the butter sticks into ½-inch slices. In a small, heavy saucepan, melt the butter pieces over the lowest setting. Add the milk chocolate chips to the melted butter, stirring constantly with a small whisk until melted. When the milk chocolate is melted and completely smooth, turn off the heat, but leave the saucepan on the burner while proceeding with the recipe.

5   Using a large whisk, lightly beat the eggs in a large mixing bowl. Place the sugars and salt in a separate small mixing bowl, then whisk into the eggs just until incorporated. Briefly whisk the melted chocolate mixture, then gradually whisk into the egg mixture until just combined. Briefly whisk in the chocolate extract and red food color.

6   Place the flour, baking powder, and cocoa powder in the small mixing bowl; whisk together to combine. Sift through a medium strainer directly onto the batter; stir in with a silicone spatula until just combined. Pour the batter into the prepared pan and spread evenly with a small offset spatula.

7   Using the pastry bag, push the pastry tip down into the brownie batter to the bottom of the pan. Pipe random dots of cheesecake batter into the brownie batter. If the cheesecake dots look "hollow" fill them in with additional cheesecake batter. The brownie batter will slightly rise in each area as you pipe in the cheesecake batter: the top of the batter will not be flat; it will even out during baking.

8   Bake for 45 minutes, until a toothpick inserted in the center of the slab comes out clean. The top of the brownie slab will be puffed when it first comes out of the oven; it will settle as it cools. Transfer the pan to a cooling rack and let cool at room temperature for 30 minutes; the cheesecake layer will continue to set up as it cools. Refrigerate the pan for 7 to 8 hours, or overnight. See page xii for instructions on removing and cutting the slab, and for refrigerated storage (up to 2 weeks) and freezing guidelines.

Polka Dot Red Velvet
Cheesecake Brownies

dulce de leche cheesecake brownies

makes 12 large squares or 24 smaller bars

I've tried to find the correct phonetic pronunciation for dulce de leche, but it seems that various cultures pronounce it differently. My lovely friend Norma, who hails from Puerto Rico, pronounces it dew-el-seh-deh-leh-cheh. You'd be appalled at how I mangled that name prior to her guidance. The brand I always use now comes in a squeeze bottle, which is much more convenient than the canned version for recipes as well as for drizzling over ice cream.

caramel rice cereal topping

Vegetable shortening for pan
¾ cup (0.07 ounce) sweetened toasted rice cereal
    (Frosted Krispies)
¼ cup (1.8 ounces) granulated sugar
1½ teaspoons water
½ teaspoon (0.01 ounce) light corn syrup
¼ teaspoon Kosher salt

brownie batter

Vegetable shortening for pan
2 sticks (8 ounces) unsalted butter
½ cup and 1 tablespoon (3 ounces) 100% cacao
    unsweetened chocolate chips
1 cup (6 ounces) 63% extra dark chocolate chips
4 large eggs, at room temperature
1 cup (7 ounces) granulated sugar
1 packed cup (8 ounces) light brown sugar
¾ teaspoon salt
1½ teaspoons pure vanilla extract
1 cup (4.5 ounces) unbleached all-purpose flour
½ teaspoon baking powder

dulce de leche cheesecake batter

1½ packages (12 ounces) cream cheese, at
    room temperature
¹⁄₃ cup and 1 tablespoon (4 ounces) dulce de leche
    (Nestlé La Lechera)
½ teaspoon salt
½ cup (4 ounces) dark brown sugar
2 tablespoon unbleached all-purpose flour
2 large eggs, at room temperature
1 teaspoon *caramel flavor
*Alternately, substitute 1 teaspoon pure
    vanilla extract

chocolate glaze

6 tablespoons (3 ounces) unsalted butter
1 tablespoon (0.08 ounce) light corn syrup
1 cup (6 ounces) 60% cacao bittersweet
    chocolate chip

1 To make the caramel rice cereal topping, lightly grease a quarter-sheet pan and line with parchment paper. Measure out the cereal; set aside. Place the sugar, water, corn syrup, and salt in a small heavy saucepan; stir with a small silicone spatula just to combine. Bring to a boil over moderately high heat. Once the mixture comes to a boil, lower the heat to medium and boil undisturbed until a dark amber-colored caramel forms, about 5 minutes. Remove the pan from the burner and stir in the rice cereal. Scrape the caramelized cereal onto the prepared pan and spread it out with a small offset spatula. Let cool at room temperature.

2 Adjust an oven rack to the middle level of the oven and preheat to 350°F. Prepare a 9 by 13-inch baking pan with heavy-duty aluminum foil as shown on page ix. Lightly grease the foil in the pan.

3 To make the brownie batter, cut the butter sticks into ½-inch slices. In a small, heavy saucepan, melt the butter pieces over the lowest setting; add the unsweetened and extra dark chocolate chips. Stir with a small whisk until combined and the chocolate is melted and smooth. Turn off the heat, but leave the saucepan on the burner while proceeding with the recipe.

4 Using a large whisk, lightly beat the eggs in a large mixing bowl. Place the sugars and salt in a separate small mixing bowl, then whisk into the eggs just until incorporated. Briefly whisk the melted chocolate mixture, then gradually whisk into the egg mixture until just combined. Briefly whisk in the vanilla. Note: Set aside the saucepan and small whisk (no need to wash them) to use later for the chocolate glaze.

5 Place the flour and baking powder in the small mixing bowl; whisk together to combine. Sift through a medium strainer directly onto the batter; stir in with a silicone spatula until just combined. Pour the batter into the prepared pan and spread evenly with a small offset spatula. Bake for 28 minutes, until a toothpick inserted in the center of the slab comes out clean. Transfer the pan to a cooling rack. Maintain the oven temperature at 350°F. Prepare the dulce de leche cheesecake batter while the brownie slab is cooling at room temperature.

6 To make the dulce de leche cheesecake batter, cut the cream cheese into 1-inch slices and place in the small mixing bowl; add the dulce de leche and salt. Using a hand mixer on high speed, beat until creamy. On medium speed, add the dark brown sugar and flour; beat an additional minute on medium speed, scraping the bowl once to make sure the mixture is perfectly smooth. Add the eggs and caramel flavor; beat on medium speed until just combined. Pour the cheesecake batter over the warm brownie slab and spread evenly with a small offset spatula. Bake an additional 15 minutes, until the cheesecake layer has very tiny cracks around the outer edges. Transfer the pan to a cooling rack and let cool at room temperature for 30 minutes; the cheesecake layer will continue to set up as it cools. Prepare the chocolate glaze.

7 To make the chocolate glaze, slice the butter into ¼-inch slices. Place the butter slices and corn syrup in the reserved small saucepan and melt over the lowest setting. Meanwhile, place the chocolate chips in a 2-cup Pyrex measuring cup. Microwave the chips on high power for 90 seconds, whisk with the reserved small whisk, then microwave an additional 15 seconds: whisk again. Pour the melted butter mixture into the melted chocolate and whisk gently until combined and completely smooth. Pour the glaze over the cheesecake layer and spread evenly with a small offset spatula.

8 Using a sharp chef's knife, cut the caramel rice cereal topping into random ¼-inch pieces. Immediately sprinkle the pieces evenly over the warm chocolate glaze. Refrigerate the pan for 7 to 8 hours, or overnight. See page xii for instructions on removing and cutting the slab, and for refrigerated storage (up to 2 weeks) and freezing guidelines.

Dulce De Leche
Cheesecake Brownies

spooky peanut butter cheesecake brownies

makes 12 large squares or 24 smaller bars

In 1997 I was the *Southern Living Cook-Off* Philadelphia Cream Cheese Brand Winner for a Peanut Butter and Chocolate Cheesecake. I've been pairing chocolate and peanut butter ever since, and whatever I come up with, it's always a hit with family and friends. I have garnished these brownies with a spooky cobweb-like design, making it an ideal treat for Halloween.

peanut butter cheesecake batter
1 (8-ounce) package cream cheese, at room temperature
½ cup (4.5 ounces) creamy peanut butter
¼ teaspoon salt
½ cup (3.5 ounces) sugar
2 large egg yolks, at room temperature
1 teaspoon pure vanilla extract

brownie batter
Vegetable shortening for pan
4 ounces (1 cup) salted large Virginia peanuts
2½ sticks (10 ounces) unsalted butter
1²/₃ cups (10 ounces) 63% extra dark chocolate chips
5 large eggs, at room temperature
2½ cups (1 pound 1.5 ounces) sugar
1 teaspoon salt
2 teaspoons pure vanilla extract
1 cup (4 ounces) cake flour
1 cup (4 ounces Dutch-processed unsweetened cocoa powder

chocolate glaze
1 stick (4 ounces) unsalted butter
1 tablespoon and 1 teaspoon (1 ounce) light corn syrup
1¹/₃ cups (8 ounces) 60% cacao bittersweet chocolate chips

peanut butter drizzle
2 teaspoons (0.03 ounce) canola oil
¹/₃ cup (2 ounces) peanut butter baking chips (Reese's)

1   Fit a medium (14-inch) pastry bag with a 3/8-inch round plain pastry tip (Ateco #804). Set aside. Note: For this recipe, I use a large pastry bag coupler so that the pastry tip extends beyond the end of the pastry bag, but a pastry bag coupler is not required.

2   To make the peanut butter cheesecake batter, cut the cream cheese into 1-inch slices and place in a small mixing bowl; add the peanut butter and salt. Using a hand mixer on high speed, beat until well

combined. On medium speed, add the sugar and beat an additional minute, scraping the bowl once to make sure the mixture is perfectly smooth. Add the egg yolks and vanilla; beat until just combined. Use a silicone spatula to dollop the peanut butter cheesecake batter into the pastry bag. Set aside.

3   Adjust an oven rack to the middle level of the oven and preheat to 350°F. Prepare a 9 by 13-inch baking pan with heavy-duty aluminum foil as shown on page ix. Lightly grease the foil in the pan.

4   Using a nut chopper or chef's knife, finely chop the peanuts. Set aside.

5   To make the brownie batter, cut the butter sticks into ½-inch slices. In a small, heavy saucepan, begin to melt the butter pieces over the lowest setting; add the extra dark chocolate chips. Stir with a small whisk until combined and the chocolate is melted and smooth. Turn off the heat, but leave the saucepan on the burner while proceeding with the recipe.

6   Using a large whisk, lightly beat the eggs in a large mixing bowl. Place the sugar and salt in a separate small mixing bowl, then whisk into the eggs just until incorporated. Briefly whisk the melted chocolate mixture, then gradually whisk into the egg mixture until just combined. Briefly whisk in the vanilla. Note: Set aside the saucepan and small whisk (no need to wash them) to use later for the chocolate glaze.

7   Place the flour and cocoa powder in the small mixing bowl; whisk together to combine. Sift through a medium strainer directly onto the batter; stir in with a silicone spatula until just combined. Sprinkle the chopped peanuts over the batter and fold in until just combined. Pour the batter into the prepared pan and spread evenly with a small offset spatula.

8   Using the pastry bag, push the pastry tip down into the brownie batter to the bottom of the pan. Pipe random dots of peanut butter cheesecake batter into the brownie batter. If the cheesecake dots look "hollow" fill them in with additional cheesecake batter. Use the tip of a finger to smooth out the top of each cheesecake mound.

9   Bake for 31 minutes, until a toothpick inserted in the center of the slab comes out clean. The top of the brownie slab will be puffed when it first comes out of the oven; it will settle as it cools. Transfer the pan to a cooling rack and let cool at room temperature for 30 minutes; the cheesecake layer will continue to set up as it cools.

10   To make the chocolate glaze, slice the butter into ¼-inch slices. Place the butter slices and corn syrup in the reserved small saucepan and melt over the lowest setting. Meanwhile, place the chocolate chips in a 2-cup Pyrex measuring cup. Microwave the chips on high power for 90 seconds, whisk with the reserved small whisk, then microwave an additional 15 seconds: whisk again. Pour the melted butter mixture into the melted chocolate and whisk gently until combined and completely smooth. Pour the glaze over the brownie slab and spread evenly with a small offset spatula.

11   To make the peanut butter drizzle, place the oil and peanut butter chips in a 1-cup glass (Pyrex) measuring cup. Microwave on 50% power for 2 minutes, then stir with a small silicone spatula until the chips are melted and completely smooth. Pour the mixture through a small plastic funnel into a small (6-ounce) plastic squeeze bottle. Squeeze the mixture over the warm glaze into random-sized concentric circles. Using the tip of a wire cake tester (or toothpick), pull lines from the center of the circles out towards the outer edge to form a spider web effect. Refrigerate the pan for 7 to 8 hours, or overnight. See page xii for instructions on removing and cutting the slab, and for refrigerated storage (up to 2 weeks) and freezing guidelines.

Spooky Peanut Butter
Cheesecake Brownies

blondies

Praline Pecan
Blondies

praline pecan blondies

makes 12 large squares or 24 smaller bars

One day I bought a plastic container of Praline Pecans at Costco, and I found my hand diving back into that container uncontrollably. I loved them so much that I knew I just had to incorporate them into a treat. The combination of those delicious praline pecans, coconut, milk chocolate, and a thick layer of caramel made for one fantastic blondie.

blondie batter
Vegetable shortening for pan
2 sticks (8 ounces) unsalted butter
2 large eggs, at room temperature
2 teaspoons pure vanilla extract
1¾ packed cups (14 ounces) light brown sugar
1 teaspoon salt
1 1/8 teaspoons baking powder
2 1/3 cups (10.5 ounces) unbleached all-purpose flour
1 cup (4 ounces) shredded sweetened coconut

caramel layer
2¼ cups (10 ounces) praline pecans (Kirkland)
3 tablespoons (1.5 ounces) unsalted butter
4½ tablespoons (2.3 ounces) heavy whipping cream
1 pound 3.5 ounces (about 66) caramel candies
   (Kraft Traditional Caramels)
1 teaspoon pure vanilla extract

milk chocolate glaze
3½ teaspoons (0.07 ounce) canola oil
1½ cups (9 ounces) milk chocolate chips

garnish
1/3 cup (1.5 ounces) praline pecans (Kirkland)

1   Adjust an oven rack to the middle level of the oven and preheat to 350°F.

2   To make the blondie batter, cut the butter sticks into ½-inch slices. Place the butter slices in a heavy 1-quart saucepan. Cook over the lowest setting until the butter melts, stirring frequently with a silicone spatula. Remove the pan from the heat and let the butter cool to lukewarm while proceeding with the recipe.

3   Prepare a 9 by 13-inch baking pan with heavy-duty aluminum foil as shown on page ix. Lightly grease the foil in the pan.

4   Place the eggs and vanilla in the bowl of a stand mixer fitted with the paddle attachment. Place the brown sugar, salt, and baking powder in a small mixing bowl, then add to the egg mixture. On medium speed, beat the mixture for 2 to 3 minutes, just until light in color and slightly thickened.

5   Reduce the mixer speed to the lowest speed and very slowly drizzle in the melted butter.

6   On the lowest speed, very gradually add the flour and beat until just combined. On low speed, gradually add the coconut and beat until just combined. Remove the bowl and paddle from the mixer stand; add any batter from the paddle to the bowl. Fold the batter with a spatula to make sure all of the ingredients are incorporated. Dollop the batter into the prepared pan and spread evenly with a small offset spatula. Bake at 350°F for 24 minutes, until a toothpick inserted in the center of the slab comes out clean and the top is nicely browned. Transfer the pan to a cooling rack. Note: Prepare the caramel layer while the blondie slab is baking.

7   To make the caramel layer, coarsely chop 10 ounces of the praline pecans by hand using a large chef's knife. Set aside.

8   Cut the butter into ¼-inch thick slices. Place the butter slices and cream in a 2-quart saucier or saucepan. Begin to melt the mixture over medium-low heat. Unwrap the caramels, and as each is unwrapped, add it to the mixture. Cook over medium-low heat, stirring occasionally with a silicone spatula, until the caramels are melted and completely smooth. Remove the pan from the heat and stir in the vanilla and chopped pecans. Pour the mixture over the baked blondie slab and spread evenly to the edges using a small offset spatula.

9   To make the milk chocolate glaze, bring a medium saucepan with two inches of water just to a boil. Place the canola oil and milk chocolate chips in a metal mixing bowl that will fit over the saucepan to form a double boiler. When the water comes to a boil, take the saucepan off the heat and place the mixing bowl over the hot water: the bottom of the metal bowl should not touch the hot water. Stir with a small silicone spatula until the chocolate is melted and perfectly smooth. Remove the mixing bowl from the saucepan and using a kitchen towel, wipe off any condensation from the bottom of the mixing bowl. Pour the chocolate evenly over the caramel layer; then spread evenly with a small offset spatula.

10 Using a nut chopper or chef's knife, finely chop the remaining praline pecans. Sprinkle the chopped pecans over the warm chocolate glaze. Refrigerate the pan for 7 to 8 hours, or overnight. See page xii for instructions on removing and cutting the slab, and for refrigerated storage (up to 2 weeks) and freezing guidelines.

nutella swirl hazelnut blondies

makes 12 large squares or 24 smaller bars

My lovely niece Tara asked me if I had a blondie using Nutella. I had several brownies in my repertoire infused with Nutella, but I never used it in a blondie. Well, I'm also a Nutella fan, so I set to work on one immediately, and the result is this bitchin' blondie!

blondie batter
Vegetable shortening for pan
3 sticks (12 ounces) unsalted butter
¾ cup (3.5 ounces) skinned and roasted whole
    hazelnuts (Nature's Garden)
2 cups (11 ounces) *milk chocolate baking wafers
    (Guittard 38%)
4 large eggs, at room temperature
2 teaspoons pure vanilla extract
1 teaspoon pure hazelnut flavoring
2½ packed cups (1 pound and 4 ounces) light
    brown sugar
1½ teaspoons salt
2 teaspoons baking powder
3⅓ cups and 2 tablespoons (15.5 ounces) unbleached
    all-purpose flour
⅓ cup (4 ounces) chocolate hazelnut spread (Nutella)
*Alternately, substitute 2 cups milk chocolate chips.

1   Adjust an oven rack to the middle level of the oven and preheat to 350°F.

2   To make the blondie batter, cut the butter sticks into ½-inch slices. Place the butter slices in a heavy 1-quart saucepan. Cook over the lowest setting until the butter melts, stirring frequently with a silicone spatula. Remove the pan from the heat and let the butter cool to lukewarm while proceeding with the recipe.

3   Prepare a 9 by 13-inch baking pan with heavy-duty aluminum foil as shown on page ix. Lightly grease the foil in the pan.

4   Using a nut chopper or chef's knife, finely chop the hazelnuts. Place in a small bowl with the milk chocolate wafers. Set aside.

5   Place the eggs, vanilla, and hazelnut flavoring in the bowl of a stand mixer fitted with the paddle attachment. Place the brown sugar, salt, and baking powder in a small mixing bowl, then add to the egg

Nutella Swirl
Hazelnut Blondies

mixture. On medium speed, beat the mixture for 2 to 3 minutes, just until light in color and slightly thickened.

6   Reduce the mixer speed to the lowest speed and very slowly drizzle in the melted butter.

7   On the lowest speed, very gradually add the flour and beat until just combined. On low speed, gradually add the chopped hazelnuts and milk chocolate wafers: beat until just combined. Remove the bowl and paddle from the mixer stand; add any batter from the paddle to the bowl. Fold the batter with a spatula to make sure all of the ingredients are incorporated. Dollop the batter into the prepared pan and spread evenly with a small offset spatula.

8   Place the Nutella in a 1-cup Pyrex measuring cup and microwave on 50% power in 30 second intervals, just until the Nutella is warm and softened. Be careful not to over-microwave the Nutella; it can scorch like chocolate. Use a teaspoon to stir the warmed Nutella until very smooth.

9   Use the teaspoon to dollop the warmed Nutella into approixmate ½-inch spots randomly over the top of the blondie batter, then gently swirl the mixtures together with the small offset spatula just through the very top layer of the blondie batter to form a marbled pattern. Bake at 350°F for 25 minutes, then reduce the oven to 325°F and bake an additional 14 minutes, until a toothpick inserted in the center of the slab comes out clean and the top is nicely browned. Transfer the pan to a cooling rack and cool at room temperature for at least 30 minutes, then refrigerate the pan for 7 to 8 hours, or overnight. See page xii for instructions on removing and cutting the slab, and for refrigerated storage (up to 2 weeks) and freezing guidelines.

chocolate-dipped caramel blondie bars

makes 24 bars

Everyone loves a good chocolate chip cookie. Sadly, that cookie is at its glorious best on the day it is made. Not so with a well made blondie! Under refrigeration in an airtight container, blondies maintain their baked perfection for several weeks; so give me a thick, chewy blondie (especially one dipped in chocolate) over a cookie any day.

blondie batter

Vegetable shortening for pan

3 sticks (12 ounces) unsalted butter

4 large eggs, at room temperature

2 teaspoons pure vanilla extract

1 teaspoon caramel flavor

2½ packed cups (1 pound and 4 ounces) light brown sugar

1½ teaspoons salt

2 teaspoons baking powder

3⅓ cups and 2 tablespoons (15.5 ounces) unbleached all-purpose flour

½ cup, tightly packed (2 ounces) sweetened coconut flakes

1 cup (6 ounces) 63% extra dark chocolate chips

⅔ cup (4 ounces) sea salt caramel chips (Hershey's)

bittersweet chocolate dip

5 teaspoons (0.07 ounce) canola oil

1 (10-ounce) package 60% cacao bittersweet chocolate chips

1   Adjust an oven rack to the middle level of the oven and preheat to 350°F.

2   Place the coconut, extra dark, and caramel chips in a small bowl; toss to combine. Set aside.

3   To make the blondie batter, cut the butter sticks into ½-inch slices. Place the butter slices in a heavy 1-quart saucepan. Cook over the lowest setting until the butter melts, stirring frequently with a silicone spatula. Remove the pan from the heat and let the butter cool to lukewarm while proceeding with the recipe.

4   Prepare a 9 by 13-inch baking pan with heavy-duty aluminum foil as shown on page ix. Lightly grease the foil in the pan.

5   Place the eggs and extracts in the bowl of a stand mixer fitted with the paddle attachment. Place the brown sugar, salt, and baking powder in a small mixing bowl, then add to the egg mixture. On medium speed, beat the mixture for 2 to 3 minutes, just until light in color and slightly thickened.

6   Reduce the mixer speed to the lowest speed and very slowly drizzle in the melted butter.

7   On the lowest speed, very gradually add the flour and beat until just combined. On low speed, gradually add the coconut and the extra dark and caramel chips: beat until just combined. Remove the bowl and paddle from the mixer stand: add any batter from the paddle to the bowl. Fold the batter with a spatula to make sure all of the ingredients are incorporated. Dollop the batter into the prepared pan and spread evenly with a small offset spatula.

8   Bake at 350°F for 25 minutes, then reduce the oven to 325°F and bake an additional 14 minutes, until a toothpick inserted in the center of the slab comes out clean and the top is nicely browned. Transfer the pan to a cooling rack and let cool at room temperature for at least 30 minutes. Refrigerate the pan for 7 to 8 hours, or overnight.

9   See page xii for instructions on removing the slab. Place the chilled slab on a cutting board and cut into 12 large squares, then cut each square in half to form 24 bars.

10 To make the bittersweet chocolate dip, place the canola oil and chocolate chips in a 1-cup Pyrex measuring cup. Microwave on high for 90 seconds, then stir with a small whisk. Continue microwaving in 15 second intervals until the chocolate is melted and smooth

11 Place two parchment lined half-sheet pans on the counter. Working with one chilled bar at a time, dip the bar vertically into the chocolate to cover half of the bar with chocolate. Drain off as much of the chocolate as possible, then place it on one of the sheet pans. Repeat with the rest of the bars. After about 10 minutes, when the chocolate starts to look set, transfer the bars to the other parchment-lined sheet pan. This step will leave the unwanted extra chocolate on the first sheet of parchment paper. Transfer the bars (still on the sheet pan) to the refrigerator until the chocolate is firm and set, at least 1 hour. See page xiv for refrigerated storage (up to 2 weeks) and freezing guidelines.

note

You will have extra melted chocolate used for dipping the blondie bars. I suggest laying out some purchased cookies (like Oreo's) close together on a half sheet pan lined with parchment paper and pouring the left over chocolate over top of the cookies. Chill until set and enjoy!

Chocolate Dipped
Caramel Blondie Bars

sea salt caramel crispy blondies

makes 12 large squares or 24 smaller bars

I'm just going to say it: adding something crispy makes everything better. This is a terrific caramel blondie, but the star of the show is the Crispy Caramel Bark on top. It is so good that I now often make it to sprinkle on top of ice cream and cupcakes, and truth be told, just to munch on by itself.

caramel crispy bark
Vegetable shortening for pan
1 tablespoon and ½ teaspoon (0.06 ounce) canola oil
1 cup (6 ounces) sea salt caramel chips (Hershey's)
1 cup (0.08 ounce) sweetened toasted rice cereal (Frosted Krispies)
½ teaspoon sea salt flakes (Maldon)

blondie batter
Vegetable shortening for pan
1½ sticks (6 ounces) unsalted butter
8 ounces sea salt caramel baking chips
5 large eggs, at room temperature
1 cup (7 ounces) granulated sugar
1 packed cup (8 ounces) dark brown sugar
¾ teaspoon salt
1 teaspoon caramel flavor
1 teaspoon pure vanilla extract
2½ cups (11.5 ounces) unbleached all-purpose flour
1 teaspoon baking powder
²/₃ cup (4 ounces) sea salt caramel chips (Hershey's)
²/₃ cup (4 ounces) 63% extra dark chocolate chips

chocolate glaze
6 tablespoons (3 ounces) unsalted butter
1 tablespoon (0.08 ounce) light corn syrup
1 cup (6 ounces) 60% cacao bittersweet chocolate chips

1   To make the caramel crispy bark, cut out a sheet of parchment paper to line the bottom of a quarter sheet pan. Lightly grease the bottom of the pan and place the parchment paper on top; press down to secure the paper onto the pan. Set aside.

2   Bring a medium saucepan with two inches of water just to a boil. Place the canola oil and caramel chips in a metal mixing bowl that will fit over the saucepan to form a double boiler. When the water comes to a boil, take the saucepan off of the heat and place the mixing bowl over the hot water; the bottom of the metal bowl should not touch the hot water. Stir with a small silicone spatula until the chips are melted and perfectly smooth. Stir in the cereal. Remove the

mixing bowl from the saucepan and using a kitchen towel, wipe off any condensation from the bottom of the mixing bowl. Scrape the caramel mixture onto the parchment-lined pan. Using a small offset spatula, spread the mixture evenly to about 1/8-inch thickness. Sprinkle the sea salt evenly over the warm caramel bark. Refrigerate the pan while proceeding with the recipe.

3   Adjust an oven rack to the middle level of the oven and preheat to 350°F. Prepare a 9 by 13-inch baking pan with heavy-duty aluminum foil as shown on page ix. Lightly grease the foil in the pan.

4   To make the blondie batter, cut the butter sticks into ½-inch slices. In a small, heavy saucepan, melt the butter pieces over the lowest setting; add the caramel chips. Stir with a small whisk until combined and the chips are melted and smooth. Turn off the heat, but leave the saucepan on the burner while proceeding with the recipe.

5   Using a large whisk, lightly beat the eggs in a large mixing bowl. Place the sugars and salt in a separate small mixing bowl, then whisk into the eggs just until incorporated. Briefly whisk the melted butter mixture (it may seem separated; that is fine), then gradually whisk into the egg mixture until just combined. Briefly whisk in the vanilla and caramel flavor. Note: Set aside the saucepan and small whisk (no need to wash them) to use later for the chocolate glaze.

6   Place the flour and baking powder in the small mixing bowl; whisk together to combine. Sift through a medium strainer directly onto the batter; stir in with a silicone spatula until just combined. Sprinkle the caramel and extra dark chips over the batter and fold in until just combined. Scrape the batter into the prepared pan and spread evenly with a small offset spatula. Bake for 32 minutes, until a toothpick inserted in the center of the slab comes out clean. Transfer the pan to a cooling rack.

7   To make the chocolate glaze, slice the butter into ¼-inch slices. Place the butter slices and corn syrup in the reserved small saucepan and melt over the lowest setting. Meanwhile, place the chocolate chips in a 2-cup Pyrex measuring cup. Microwave the chips on high power for 90 seconds, whisk with the reserved small whisk, then microwave an additional 15 seconds: whisk again. Pour the melted butter mixture into the melted chocolate and whisk gently until combined and completely smooth. Pour the glaze over the warm blondie slab and spread evenly with a small offset spatula. Place the pan in the refrigerator for 20 minutes to cool down the glaze. Note: Chop the caramel crispy bark while the glaze is cooling.

8   Using the parchment paper, transfer the chilled bark to a cutting board. Using a large chef's knife, coarsely chop the bark into approixmate ¼-inch dice. Place the chopped bark in a small bowl and place in the freezer to chill while the glaze continues to cool in the refrigerator.

9   Sprinkle the chopped bark evenly over the chocolate glaze, then using the back of a metal spatula, lightly tap on the bark to slightly imbed it into the glaze. Refrigerate the pan for 7 to 8 hours, or overnight. See page xii for instructions on removing and cutting the slab, and for refrigerated storage (up to 2 weeks) and freezing guidelines.

Sea Salt Caramel
Crispy Blondies

rockin' rum raisin blondies

makes 12 large squares or 24 smaller bars

Some people are crazy about Rum Raisin ice cream. I don't happen to be one of them, but I am crazy about these blondies. Loaded with golden raisins that have been plumped with dark rum, this sophisticated chewie blondie is geared towards adults, but kids love them too.

blondie batter

Vegetable shortening for pan
1 packed cup (5 ounces) golden raisins
1 tablespoon dark rum
3 sticks (12 ounces) unsalted butter
4 large eggs, at room temperature
2 teaspoons rum extract
1 teaspoon pure vanilla extract
2½ packed cups (1 pound 4 ounces) light brown sugar
1½ teaspoons salt
2 teaspoons baking powder
3^1/$_3$ cups and 2 tablespoons (15.5 ounces) unbleached all-purpose flour

shiny chocolate ganache

1 cup (6 ounces) semisweet chocolate chips
^{2}/$_3$ cup (4 ounces) milk chocolate chips
4 teaspoons (0.06 ounce) unsalted butter
½ cup and 2 tablespoons (5 ounces) heavy whipping cream

garnish

1 (3.5-ounce) box dark chocolate covered raisins (Raisinets)

1   Place the raisins in a small bowl, then drizzle with the dark rum. Using a silicone spatula, fold the raisins to coat with the rum. Set aside.

2   Adjust an oven rack to the middle level of the oven and preheat to 350°F.

3   To make the blondie batter, cut the butter sticks into ½-inch slices. Place the butter slices in a heavy 1-quart saucepan. Cook over the lowest setting until the butter melts, stirring frequently with a silicone spatula. Remove the pan from the heat and let the butter cool to lukewarm while proceeding with the recipe.

4   Prepare a 9 by 13-inch baking pan with heavy-duty aluminum foil as shown on page ix. Lightly grease the foil in the pan.

5   Place the eggs and extracts in the bowl of a stand mixer fitted with the paddle attachment. Place the brown sugar, salt, and baking powder in a small mixing bowl, then add to the egg mixture. On medium speed, beat the mixture for 2 to 3 minutes, just until light in color and slightly thickened.

115

6 Reduce the mixer speed to the lowest speed and very slowly drizzle in the melted butter. Note: Set aside the saucepan (no need to wash it) to use later for the chocolate ganache.

7 On the lowest speed, very gradually add the flour and beat until just combined. On low speed, gradually add the plumped raisins: beat until just combined. Remove the bowl and paddle from the mixer stand: add any batter from the paddle to the bowl. Fold the batter with a spatula to make sure all of the ingredients are incorporated. Dollop the batter into the prepared pan and spread evenly with a small offset spatula.

8 Bake at 350°F for 25 minutes, then reduce the oven to 325°F and bake an additional 15 minutes, until a toothpick inserted in the center of the slab comes out clean and the top is nicely browned. Transfer the pan to a cooling rack.

9 To make the shiny chocolate ganache, place the semisweet and the milk chocolate chips in a small bowl; set aside. Cut the butter into tiny (1/8-inch) dice; set aside.

10 Bring the cream just to a simmer over medium-high heat in the reserved saucepan. Remove the pan from the heat and add the chocolate chips; shake the pan to cover the chips with the hot cream. Cover the pan tightly and let sit off the heat for 2 minutes.

11 Add the butter bits, then place the pan back on the burner (heat turned off) and gently blend the mixture together with a small whisk just until the chips and butter are melted and incorporated into a shiny,

smooth ganache. Pour the ganache over the warm slab and spread evenly with a small offset spatula. Place the pan in the refrigerator for 15 minutes to slightly cool down the ganache.

12 Place the chocolate covered raisins evenly over the chocolate ganache. Refrigerate the pan for 7 to 8 hours, or overnight. See page xii for instructions on removing and cutting the slab, and for refrigerated storage (up to 2 weeks) and freezing guidelines.

Rockin' Rum
Raisin Blondies

hiker's cranberry oatmeal blondies

makes 12 large squares or 24 smaller bars

Let's talk about dried cranberries. The most frequently found brand in your grocery store has two ingredients: cranberries and cane sugar. They have eliminated the tartness and actual flavor of cranberries. I recommend Vincent Dried Cranberries, which are infused with unsweetened apple juice. They have a perfect amount of tartness and are a little bit chewier, which I consider a plus for this terrific blondie that is perfect for hikers, bikers, and any other outdoor activity.

blondie batter
Vegetable shortening for pan
3 sticks (12 ounces) unsalted butter
4 large eggs, at room temperature
2 teaspoons pure vanilla extract
¼ teaspoon pure almond extract
2½ packed cups (1 pound and 4 ounces) light
   brown sugar
1½ teaspoons salt
2 teaspoons baking powder
2 teaspoons ground cinnamon
3⅓ cups and 2 tablespoons (15.5 ounces) unbleached
   all-purpose flour
1 (9.5-ounce) package dried cranberries, divided (Vincent)
1 cup (3 ounces) old fashioned oats

1   Adjust an oven rack to the middle level of the oven and preheat to 350°F.

2   To make the blondie batter, cut the butter sticks into ½-inch slices. Place the butter slices in a heavy 1-quart saucepan. Cook over the lowest setting until the butter melts, stirring frequently with a silicone spatula. Remove the pan from the heat and let the butter cool to lukewarm while proceeding with the recipe.

3   Prepare a 9 by 13-inch baking pan with heavy-duty aluminum foil as shown on page ix. Lightly grease the foil in the pan.

4   Place the eggs and extracts in the bowl of a stand mixer fitted with the paddle attachment. Place the brown sugar, salt, baking powder, and cinnamon in a small mixing bowl, then add to the egg mixture. On medium speed, beat the mixture for 2 to 3 minutes, just until light in color and slightly thickened.

Hiker's Cranberry
Oatmeal Blondies

5   Reduce the mixer speed to the lowest speed and very slowly drizzle in the melted butter.

6   On the lowest speed, very gradually add the flour and beat until just combined.

7   Set aside 3 tablespoons (1 ounce) of the cranberries to use as garnish. On low speed, gradually add the remaining cranberries and oats and beat until just combined. Remove the bowl and paddle from the mixer stand; add any batter from the paddle to the bowl. Fold the batter with a spatula to make sure all of the ingredients are incorporated. Dollop the batter into the prepared pan and spread evenly with a small offset spatula. Dot the top of the slab with the reserved cranberries.

8   Bake at 350°F for 25 minutes, then reduce the oven to 325°F and bake an additional 15 minutes, until a toothpick inserted in the center of the slab comes out clean and the top is nicely browned. Transfer the pan to a cooling rack and let cool at room temperature for at least 15 minutes. Refrigerate the pan for 7 to 8 hours, or overnight. See page xii for instructions on removing and cutting the slab, and for refrigerated storage (up to 2 weeks) and freezing guidelines.

teddy bear s'more blondies

makes 12 large squares

Like a good s'more, these blondies are best eaten right after the marshmallow layer has been toasted with a torch and garnished with graham cracker teddy bears and mini milk chocolate candy bars. I brought a tray of these out at a recent picnic and the kids went crazy!

blondie batter
Vegetable shortening for pan
2 sticks (8 ounces) unsalted butter
2 large eggs, at room temperature
2 teaspoons pure vanilla extract
¼ teaspoon pure almond extract
1¾ cups, firmly packed (14 ounces) light brown sugar
1 teaspoon salt
$1^{1}/_{8}$ teaspoons baking powder
1 teaspoon ground cinnamon
$2^{1}/_{3}$ cups (10.5 ounces) unbleached all-purpose flour
1 (10-ounce) package chocolate chunks or chips
1 (16-ounce) bag miniature marshmallows

garnish
2 (3.6-ounce/8 bars each) packages Hershey's milk
    chocolate mini candy bars
1 (10-ounce) box Honey Teddy Grahams (Nabisco)

1   Adjust an oven rack to the middle level of the oven and preheat to 350°F.

2   To make the blondie batter, cut the butter sticks into ½-inch slices. Place the butter slices in a heavy 1-quart saucepan. Cook over the lowest setting until the butter melts, stirring frequently with a silicone spatula. Remove the pan from the heat and let the butter cool to lukewarm while proceeding with the recipe.

3   Prepare a 9 by 13-inch baking pan with heavy-duty aluminum foil as shown on page ix. Lightly grease the foil in the pan.

4   Place the eggs and extracts in the bowl of a stand mixer fitted with the paddle attachment. Place the brown sugar, salt, baking powder, and cinnamon in a small mixing bowl, then add to the egg mixture. On medium speed, beat the mixture for 2 to 3 minutes, just until light in color and slightly thickened.

5   Reduce the mixer speed to the lowest speed and very slowly drizzle in the melted butter.

Teddy Bear S'more
Blondies

6   On the lowest speed, very gradually add the flour and beat until just combined. On low speed, gradually add the chocolate chunks and beat until just combined. Remove the bowl and paddle from the mixer stand; add any batter from the paddle to the bowl. Fold the batter with a spatula to make sure all of the ingredients are incorporated. Dollop the batter into the prepared pan and spread evenly with a small offset spatula. Bake for 26 minutes, until a toothpick inserted in the center of the slab comes out clean and the top is nicely browned, then remove the pan from the oven and sprinkle the marshmallows evenly over the blondie slab. Return the pan to the oven and bake an additional 4 minutes, until the marshmallows are puffed, but not browned. Transfer the pan to a cooling rack. Let the slab sit at room temperature for at least 15 minutes, then refrigerate the pan for 7 to 8 hours, or overnight.

7   After the slab has been well chilled, see page xii for instructions on removing and cutting the slab into 12 large squares.

8   Using a sharp chef's knife, cut the chocolate bars into small pieces, using the grooves on the candy bars as a guideline as to where to cut. Pour a handful of the Teddy Grahams into a small bowl.

9   Working with two blondies at a time, use a propane torch to lightly brown the marshmallow topping. To best do this, the torch should be moved rapidly over the surface of the marshmallows: the flame should never rest directly on the marshmallows. If a marshmallow should flame up, quickly blow it out. When the torching is done, push five pieces of milk chocolate and four Teddy Grahams onto each blondie. Repeat the process with the remaining blondies. See page xiv for refrigerated storage (up to 2 weeks) and freezing guidelines.

triple threat peanut butter blondies

makes 12 large squares or 24 smaller bars

These are for peanut lovers, and I just assume that's everyone who is not allergic to peanuts. This outlandish treat has loads of chopped peanuts in a peanut butter blondie topped with quartered peanut butter cups. 'Nuf said?

blondie batter
Vegetable shortening and 2 teaspoons flour for pan
2 sticks (8 ounces) unsalted butter
1½ cups (13.5 ounces) creamy peanut butter (Jif)
1½ cups (6 ounces) roasted salted Virginia peanuts
4 large eggs, at room temperature
2 teaspoons pure vanilla extract
1½ cups (10.5) ounces granulated sugar
1½ cups (12 ounces) dark brown sugar
1¼ teaspoons salt
2 teaspoons baking powder
2½ cups (11.3 ounces) unbleached all-purpose flour

milk chocolate glaze
5 teaspoons (0.07 ounce) canola oil
1½ cups (9 ounces) milk chocolate chips

garnish
1 (7.6-ounce) package unwrapped mini peanut
    butter cups (Reese's)

1   Adjust an oven rack to the middle level of the oven and preheat to 350 F.

2   To make the blondie batter, cut the butter sticks into ½-inch slices and place in a small, heavy saucepan. Add the peanut butter to the saucepan: the easiest way to do this is by weight. Place the saucepan on a scale, tare off (subtract) the weight of the pan and butter, and add the correct weight of peanut butter directly into the saucepan from the jar. Melt together over the lowest setting, stirring occasionally with a small whisk until the mixture is melted and smooth. Remove the pan from the heat and let the mixture cool to lukewarm while proceeding with the recipe.

3   Prepare a 9 by 13-inch baking pan with heavy-duty aluminum foil as shown on page ix. Lightly grease the foil in the pan, then dust the interior bottom and sides of the pan with 2 teaspoons of flour. Knock out excess flour onto a sheet of newspaper for easy clean up.

4   Using a nut chopper or chef's knife, finely chop the peanuts. Set aside.

5   Place the eggs and vanilla in the bowl of a stand mixer fitted with the paddle attachment. Place the sugars, salt, and baking powder in a small mixing bowl, then add to the egg mixture. On medium speed, beat the mixture for 2 to 3 minutes, just until light in color and slightly thickened.

6   Reduce the mixer speed to the lowest speed and very slowly drizzle in the melted butter/peanut butter mixture.

7   On the lowest speed, very gradually add the flour and beat until just combined. On low speed, gradually add the chopped peanuts and beat until just combined. Remove the bowl and paddle from the mixer stand; add any batter from the paddle to the bowl. Fold the batter with a spatula to make sure all of the ingredients are incorporated. Dollop the batter into the prepared pan and spread evenly with a small offset spatula. Bake at 350°F for 30 minutes, then lower the oven temperature to 325°F and bake an additional 10 minutes, until a toothpick inserted in the center of the slab comes out clean and the top is nicely browned. Transfer the pan to a cooling rack.

8   To make the milk chocolate glaze, bring a medium saucepan with two inches of water just to a boil. Place the canola oil and milk chocolate chips in a metal mixing bowl that will fit over the saucepan to form a double boiler. When the water comes to a boil, take the saucepan off the burner and place the mixing bowl over the hot water: the bottom of the metal bowl should not touch the hot water. Stir with a small silicone spatula until the chocolate is melted and perfectly smooth. Remove the mixing bowl from the saucepan and using a kitchen towel, wipe off any condensation from the bottom of the mixing bowl. Pour the glaze over the top of the warm blondie slab and spread evenly with a small offset spatula. Place the pan in the refrigerator for 20 minutes to cool down the glaze.

9   While the milk chocolate glaze is cooling, cut the mini peanut butter cups into quarters. Place the peanut butter cup pieces in a small bowl and place in the freezer to chill while the glaze is cooling for 20 minutes in the refrigerator.

10 Sprinkle the quartered mini peanut butter cups evenly over the milk chocolate glaze. Refrigerate the pan for 7 to 8 hours, or overnight. See page xii for instructions on removing and cutting the slab, and for refrigerated storage (up to 2 weeks) and freezing guidelines.

Triple Threat
Peanut Butter Blondies

whole lotta colada blondies

makes 12 large squares or 24 smaller bars

Remember that old song that asked the question "if you like pina coladas?" Well, I don't like pina coladas, but I sure do like all of the ingredients that go into one, so I incorporated them into a white chocolate blondie. This a virgin version: no rum.

blondie batter

Vegetable shortening for pan

2 cups (8 ounces) sweetened coconut flakes

1¼ cups (6 ounces) *sweetened dried pineapple chunks

1½ sticks (6 ounces) unsalted butter

6 ounces premium white baking chocolate

4 large eggs, at room temperature

2 cups (14 ounces) sugar

1 teaspoon salt

1 teaspoon pure vanilla extract

1 teaspoon coconut extract

2½ cups (11.5 ounces) unbleached all-purpose flour

½ teaspoon baking powder

Often found in grocery stores in clear plastic containers with other dried fruits and nuts

pineapple cream cheese frosting

1 (8-ounce) package cream cheese, at room temperature

6 tablespoons (3 ounces) unsalted butter, at
room temperature

¼ teaspoon salt

2 tablespoons (1 ounce) pineapple juice (fresh or canned)

½ teaspoon pure vanilla extract

½ teaspoon pineapple extract (or flavor)

3 drops yellow food color (optional)

1½ cups (6 ounces) confectioners' sugar

1. Adjust an oven rack to the middle level of the oven and preheat to 350°F. Spread the coconut out evenly onto a half-sheet pan. Bake for 5 minutes, then turn the coconut with a metal spatula, bringing it from the outer edges of the pan into the center. Bake for 3 additional minutes; repeat turning the coconut, then continue to bake in 2 minute intervals, turning the coconut until the coconut is uniformly golden brown with just a bit of darker coconut color. Transfer the pan to a cooling rack and let cool at room temperature. Maintain the oven temperature at 350°F.

2. While the coconut is toasting, use a chef's knife to cut the dried pineapple chunks into approixmate ¼-inch dice. Set aside.

3. Prepare a 9 by 13-inch baking pan with heavy-duty aluminum foil as shown on page ix. Lightly grease the foil in the pan. To make the blondie batter, cut the butter sticks into ½-inch slices. In a small, heavy saucepan, melt the butter pieces over the lowest setting. While the butter is melting, chop the white chocolate very finely and add to the melted butter. Stir with a small whisk until combined and the white chocolate is melted and smooth. Remove the pan from the heat and set aside.

Whole Lotta Colada
Blondies

4   Using a large whisk, lightly beat the eggs in a large mixing bowl. Place the sugar and salt in a separate small mixing bowl, then whisk into the eggs just until incorporated. Briefly whisk the melted white chocolate mixture, then gradually whisk into the egg mixture until just combined. Briefly whisk in the extracts.

5   Place the flour and baking powder in the small mixing bowl; whisk together to combine. Sift through a medium strainer directly onto the batter; stir in with a silicone spatula until just combined.

6   Set aside ¾-cup (1.5 ounces) of the toasted coconut to use later for garnish. Sprinkle the remaining toasted coconut and the chopped dried pineapple over the batter and fold in until just combined. Scrape the batter into the prepared pan and spread evenly with a small offset spatula. Bake for 30 minutes, until a toothpick inserted in the center of the slab comes out clean and the top is nicely browned. Transfer the pan to a cooling rack set in the freezer to quickly cool the top of the blondie slab before covering it with the pineapple cream cheese frosting.

7   To make the pineapple cream cheese frosting, place the cream cheese, butter, and salt in a small mixing bowl. Using a hand mixer on high speed, beat the mixture until it is light and fluffy. Reduce the speed to low and beat in the pineapple juice, the extracts, and yellow food color until well combined. Add the confectioners' sugar to the bowl (no need to sift) and starting on low and gradually increasing to high, beat until creamy and smooth. Dollop the frosting over the chilled blondie slab and spread evenly with a small offset spatula. Sprinkle the reserved toasted coconut evenly over the frosting, then use the back of a metal spatula to lightly tap on the coconut to slightly imbed it into the frosting. Refrigerate the pan for 7 to 8 hours, or overnight. See page xii for instructions on removing and cutting the slab, and for refrigerated storage (up to 2 weeks) and freezing guidelines.

chock full of cherries blondies

makes 12 large squares or 24 smaller bars

I created this blondie for my sweetheart, my husband Don, who loves all things cherry. We have several Montmorency sour cherry trees in our yard, but apparently they don't like it here in Virginia Beach, since they rarely produce enough cherries each summer for even one pie. The combination of luscious cream cheese frosting swirled with cherry filling on top makes this blondie taste like a terrific cheesecake: maybe better!

blondie batter

Vegetable shortening for pan
1 (5-ounce) package dried tart cherries (Stoneridge Orchards)
1 teaspoon canola oil
1½ sticks (6 ounces) unsalted butter
6 ounces premium white baking chocolate
4 large eggs, at room temperature
2 cups (14 ounces) sugar
1 teaspoon salt
2 teaspoons pure vanilla extract
2½ cups (11.5 ounces) unbleached all-purpose flour
½ teaspoon baking powder
2 (12-ounce) cans *cherry cake and pastry filling (Solo), divided
*Alternately, use a good quality cherry jam.

cream cheese frosting

8 ounces (1 package) cream cheese, at room temperature
1 stick (4 ounces) unsalted butter, at room temperature
½ teaspoon salt
1 pound confectioners' sugar
1 teaspoon pure vanilla extract
1 teaspoon clear vanilla extract

1   Adjust an oven rack to the middle level of the oven and preheat to 350°F. Prepare a 9 by 13-inch baking pan with heavy-duty aluminum foil as shown on page ix. Lightly grease the foil in the pan.

2   Place the tart cherries in the small mixing bowl; add the canola oil. Toss the cherries and canola oil together to coat the cherries; having a bit of oil on the cherries makes them stick less to the blade of your knife as you chop. Turn the cherries out onto a cutting board and coarsely chop them using a chef's knife. Set aside.

3   To make the blondie batter, cut the butter sticks into ½-inch slices. In a small, heavy saucepan, melt the butter pieces over the lowest setting. While the butter is melting, chop the white chocolate very finely and add to the melted butter. Stir with a small whisk until combined and the white chocolate is melted and smooth. Remove the pan from the heat and set aside.

4. Using a large whisk, lightly beat the eggs in a large mixing bowl. Place the sugar and salt in a separate small mixing bowl, then whisk into the eggs just until incorporated. Briefly whisk the melted chocolate mixture, then gradually whisk into the egg mixture until just combined. Briefly whisk in the vanilla.

5. Place the flour and baking powder in the small mixing bowl; whisk together to combine. Sift through a medium strainer directly onto the batter; stir in with a silicone spatula until just combined. Sprinkle the chopped cherries over the batter and fold in until just combined.

6. Scrape half (1 pound 8 ounces) of the blondie batter into the prepared pan. The best way to do this is by weight. Place the prepared pan on a scale, tare off (subtract) the weight of the pan, and scrape the correct weight of batter directly into the pan. Spread the batter evenly with a small offset spatula. Bake for 20 minutes, until a toothpick inserted near the center of the slab comes out clean and the top is nicely browned. Transfer the pan to a cooling rack.

7. Open the cans of cherry filling and set aside ½ cup (5 ounces) from one of the cans to use later as garnish. Spoon the remaining cherry filling (from both cans) evenly over the baked first layer of the blondie, then spread evenly with a small offset spatula. Dollop the remaining blondie batter evenly over the cherry filling and carefully spread to the edges with the offset spatula, covering the cherry filling. Bake for 28 minutes, until a toothpick inserted in the center of the slab comes out clean and the top is nicely browned. Transfer the pan to a cooling rack set in the refrigerator. Chill the slab in the pan until the top of the slab is cool, at least 1 hour.

8. To make the cream cheese frosting, place the cream cheese, butter, and salt in the bowl of a stand mixer fitted with the paddle attachment. Beat on medium-high speed until light and fluffy. On low speed, gradually add the confectioners' sugar (no need to sift) until just incorporated; do not overbeat. On low speed add the vanilla extracts; beat until just incorporated, then increase the mixer speed to medium-high and beat for 10 seconds. Scrape down the sides of the bowl then beat again briefly. Dollop the frosting over the chilled blondie slab and spread evenly with a small offset spatula.

9. Use a teaspoon to spoon the cherry filling into approixmate 1-inch spots randomly over the top of the cream cheese frosting, then lightly swirl the mixtures together with a cake tester (or toothpick) to form a marbled pattern. Refrigerate the pan for 7 to 8 hours, or overnight. See page xii for instructions on removing and cutting the slab, and for refrigerated storage (up to 2 weeks) and freezing guidelines.

Chock Full Of Cherries
Blondies

coconut cookie blondies

makes 12 large squares or 24 smaller bars

I know what you're thinking: why should I make this bark to use inside the blondies when I could just use chocolate chips? Well, you can, but here's the thing: the coconut cookie chocolate bark adds a little crunch that you miss out on with chocolate chips. Plus, you get delightful streaks of chocolate shooting through the blondies. Note: If you prefer not to make the coconut cookie chocolate bark, substitute 1½ cups (9 ounces) of bittersweet chocolate chips or chunks instead.

coconut cookie chocolate bark
Vegetable shortening for pan
3 teaspoons (0.04 ounce) canola oil
1 cup (6 ounces) 60% cacao bittersweet chocolate chips
12 cookies (about 2 ounces) toasted coconut cookie thins (Mrs. Thinsters)

blondie batter
Vegetable shortening for pan
1 cup (2.8 ounces) organic unsweetened shredded coconut (Let's Do Organic)
2 sticks (8 ounces) unsalted butter
10 ounces premium white baking chocolate
5 large eggs, at room temperature
2½ cups (1 pound and 1.5 ounces) sugar
1 teaspoon salt
2 teaspoons pure vanilla extract
1 teaspoon coconut extract
3½ cups (15.8 ounces) unbleached all-purpose flour
1 teaspoon baking powder

1 To make the coconut cookie chocolate bark, cut out a sheet of parchment paper to line the bottom of an *eighth-size sheet pan. Lightly grease the bottom of the pan and place the parchment paper on top; press down to secure the paper onto the pan. Set aside. *Alternately, line a quarter-sheet pan with parchment and only spread the bark mixture onto half of the pan.

2 Bring a medium saucepan with two inches of water just to a boil. Place the canola oil and chocolate chips in a metal mixing bowl that will fit over the saucepan to form a double boiler. When the water comes to a boil, take the saucepan off the heat and place the mixing bowl over the hot water: the bottom of the metal bowl should not touch the hot water. Stir with a small silicone spatula until the chocolate is melted and perfectly smooth.

3 Use a chef's knife to cut the cookies into ½-inch dice, then sprinkle the chopped cookies over the melted

chocolate: stir with the spatula to coat the cookie pieces. Remove the mixing bowl from the saucepan and using a kitchen towel, wipe off any condensation from the bottom of the mixing bowl. Scrape the mixture onto the parchment-lined pan. Using a small offset spatula, spread the chocolate mixture evenly to cover the bottom of the prepared pan. Place the pan in the freezer while proceeding with the recipe.

4   Adjust an oven rack to the middle level of the oven and preheat to 350 F. Prepare a 9 by 13-inch baking pan with heavy-duty aluminum foil as shown on page ix.

5   Spread the unsweetened coconut out evenly onto a quarter-sheet pan. Bake for 3 to 4 minutes; the coconut should be a golden color. Transfer the pan to a cooling rack. Maintain the oven temperature at 350°F.

6   To make the blondie batter, cut the butter sticks into ½-inch slices. In a small, heavy saucepan, melt the butter pieces over the lowest setting. While the butter is melting, chop the white chocolate very finely and add to the melted butter. Stir with a small whisk until combined and the white chocolate is melted and smooth. Remove the pan from the heat and set aside.

7   Using a large whisk, lightly beat the eggs in a large mixing bowl. Place the sugar and salt in a separate small mixing bowl, then whisk into the eggs just until incorporated. Briefly whisk the melted white chocolate mixture, then gradually whisk into the egg mixture until just combined. Briefly whisk in the extracts.

8   Place the flour and baking powder in the small mixing bowl; whisk together to combine. Sift through a medium strainer directly onto the batter; stir in with a silicone spatula until just combined.

9   Turn the chilled bark out onto a cutting board. Using a large chef's knife, chop the bark into ½-inch dice. Sprinkle the toasted coconut and the chopped bark over the batter and fold in until just combined. Dollop the batter into the prepared pan and spread evenly with a small offset spatula. Bake at 350°F for 35 minutes, until a toothpick inserted in the center of the slab comes out clean and the top is nicely browned. Transfer the pan to a cooling rack and let cool at room temperature for at least 15 minutes, then refrigerate the pan for 7 to 8 hours, or overnight. See page xii for instructions on removing and cutting the slab, and for refrigerated storage (up to 2 weeks) and freezing guidelines.

Coconut Cookie Blondies

spring fling white chocolate blondies

makes 12 large squares or 24 smaller bars

I created this pretty blondie with Spring in mind. Cut into small squares, it's perfect for an Easter brunch and also works well for baby showers. Of course, you can substitute other candies in the blondie as well as for the garnish on top, but if you opt for the candies I used, both are seasonal items, so stock up on them when they show up in your grocery store.

blondie batter
Vegetable shortening for pan
1½ sticks (6 ounces) unsalted butter
6 ounces premium white baking chocolate
4 large eggs, at room temperature
2 cups (14 ounces) sugar
1 teaspoon salt
2 teaspoons pure vanilla extract
2½ cups (11.5 ounces) unbleached all-purpose flour
½ teaspoon baking powder
2 cups (12 ounces) milk chocolate mini eggs (Cadbury)

vanilla banache
½ cup (4 ounces) heavy whipping cream
2¹⁄₃ cups (14 ounces) classic white chips (Ghirardelli)

garnish
¼ cup (1.5 ounces) pastel milk chocolate sunflower
    seeds (JUST for FUN)

1   Adjust an oven rack to the middle level of the oven and preheat to 350°F. Prepare a 9 by 13-inch baking pan with heavy-duty aluminum foil as shown on page ix. Lightly grease the foil in the pan.

2   To make the blondie batter, cut the butter sticks into ½-inch slices. In a small, heavy saucepan, melt the butter pieces over the lowest setting. While the butter is melting, chop the white chocolate very finely and add to the melted butter. Stir with a small whisk until combined and the white chocolate is melted and smooth. Remove the pan from the heat and set aside.

Spring Fling
White Chocolate Blondies

3   Using a large whisk, lightly beat the eggs in a large mixing bowl. Place the sugar and salt in a separate small mixing bowl, then whisk into the eggs just until incorporated. Briefly whisk the melted white chocolate mixture, then gradually whisk into the egg mixture until just combined. Briefly whisk in the vanilla. Note: Set aside the saucepan (no need to wash it) to use later for the vanilla ganache.

4   Place the flour and baking powder in the small mixing bowl; whisk together to combine. Sift through a medium strainer directly onto the batter; stir in with a silicone spatula until just combined. Dollop half (1 pound 6 ounces) of the blondie batter into the prepared pan. The best way to do this is by weight. Place the prepared pan on a scale, tare off (subtract) the weight of the pan, and scrape the correct weight of batter directly into the pan. Spread the batter evenly with a small offset spatula. Sprinkle the mini eggs evenly over the batter. Dollop the remaining blondie batter over the mini eggs and spread evenly with a small offset spatula, taking care to cover the mini eggs completely. Bake for 34 minutes, until a toothpick inserted in the center of the slab comes out clean and the top is nicely browned. Transfer the pan to a cooling rack.

5   To make the vanilla ganache, place the white chips in a small bowl. Set aside.

6   Place the cream in the reserved saucepan. Bring the cream just to a simmer; do not let it boil. Take the pan off of the heat and add the white chips. Shake the pan slightly to cover the chips with the cream. Cover the pan with a lid and let sit for 2 minutes. Return the pan to the burner (with the heat turned off) and blend together with a small silicone spatula just until the chips are incorporated and completely melted. Pour the ganache over the warm blondie slab and spread evenly with a small offset spatula. Place the chocolate sunflower seeds over the warm ganache, slightly pushing them into the ganache. Refrigerate the pan for 7 to 8 hours, or overnight. See page xii for instructions on removing and cutting the slab, and for refrigerated storage (up to 2 weeks) and freezing guidelines.

confetti cookies n' cream blondies

makes 12 large squares or 24 smaller bars

You may think these Confetti Blondies are named after the confetti sprinkles on top, but the word "confetti" for me will always be associated with my trusty dappled gray mare Confetti, who was an excellent trail horse. She would jump any ditch or obstacle, as long as the braver (and better trained) horse in front of her did it first. At the time I baked these for the photo shoot, I used colorful "Lady Gaga" Oreo limited edition cookies, but always available Golden Oreos are the standard cookie for this blondie.

blondie batter
Vegetable shortening for pan
2 sticks (8 ounces) unsalted butter
2 large eggs, at room temperature
2 teaspoons pure vanilla extract
1¾ cups, firmly packed (14 ounces) light brown sugar
1 teaspoon salt
$1^{1}/_{8}$ teaspoons baking powder
$2^{1}/_{3}$ cups (10.5 ounces) unbleached all-purpose flour
20 Golden Oreo cookies from 1 (14.3-ounce) package

fluffy white frosting
8 tablespoons (3.2 ounces) white all-vegetable shortening
1 stick (4 ounces) unsalted butter, at room temperature
1 cup (4.8 ounces) marshmallow fluff (or creme)
2 teaspoons pure vanilla bean paste (or pure vanilla extract)
1 teaspoon clear imitation vanilla extract
1¼ cups (5 ounces) confectioners' sugar

cookie garnish
1¼ cups (4 ounces) Golden Oreo minis

white chip drizzle
1 tablespoon (.04 ounce) canola oil
$^{1}/_{3}$ cup (2 ounces) white baking chips (Guittard Choc-Au-Lait)

candy garnish
1 tablespoon Confetti Pastel Sequins (CK Products)

1. Adjust an oven rack to the middle level of the oven and preheat to 350°F.

2. To make the blondie batter, cut the butter sticks into ½-inch slices. Place the butter slices in a heavy 1-quart saucepan. Cook over the lowest setting until the butter melts, stirring frequently with a silicone spatula. Remove the pan from the heat and let the butter cool to lukewarm while proceeding with the recipe.

3. Cut out a sheet of parchment paper to measure 9½ x 13½ inches. Lightly grease the bottom and interior sides of a 9 by 13-inch baking pan with a *removable bottom. Place the parchment paper on the bottom of the pan to come ¼-inch up the sides of the pan. Lightly grease the parchment paper. Set aside. Note: If you don't have a pan with a removable bottom, prepare a standard 9 by 13-inch baking pan with foil as directed on page ix.

4. Place the eggs and vanilla in the bowl of a stand mixer fitted with the paddle attachment. Place the brown sugar, salt, and baking powder in a small mixing bowl, then add to the egg mixture. On medium speed, beat the mixture for 2 to 3 minutes, just until light in color and slightly thickened.

5. Reduce the mixer speed to the lowest speed and very slowly drizzle in the melted butter.

6. On the lowest speed, very gradually add the flour and beat until just combined. Remove the bowl and paddle from the mixer stand; add any batter from the paddle to the bowl. Fold the batter with a spatula to make sure all of the ingredients are incorporated. Dollop the batter into the prepared pan and spread evenly with a small offset spatula. Push the Oreo cookies into the batter; do not place any within ½-inch of the pan sides. Use the offset spatula to cover the cookies with the batter. Bake for

30 minutes, until a toothpick inserted in the center of the slab comes out clean and the top is nicely browned. Transfer the pan to a cooling rack and let cool at room temperature for 10 minutes, then place the pan in the freezer for 20 minutes to cool down the blondie slab.

7. To make the fluffy white frosting, using a stand mixer fitted with the paddle attachment, beat together the shortening and butter on medium speed until well combined. Add the marshmallow fluff and vanilla extracts to the mixing bowl and beat on medium-low speed until well combined. Add the confectioners' sugar (no need to sift) to the mixer bowl. Starting on low speed and gradually increasing to medium-high, beat until the mixture is fluffy, about 1 minute. Scrape down the sides of the bowl and beat again briefly. Dollop the frosting over the blondie slab and spread evenly with a small offset spatula, then immediately garnish with the mini Oreos, slightly pushing them into the frosting with your fingertips.

8. To make the white chip drizzle, pour the oil into a 1-cup Pyrex measuring cup; add the white chips. Microwave on 50% power for 2 minutes, then stir with a small silicone spatula until the chips are melted and completely smooth. Using the spatula, drizzle random stripes liberally over the top of the blondie slab. Sprinkle the confetti sequins evenly over the drizzle. Refrigerate the pan for 7 to 8 hours, or overnight.

9. To remove the blondie slab from the pan, run a thin knife between the slab and the sides of the pan. Push the bottom of the pan up out of the sides and place it on a cutting board. Use a long chef's knife to cut it into 12 large squares, cleaning the knife in hot water and drying before each cut to provide sharp clean edges. See page xiv for refrigerated storage (up to 2 weeks) and freezing guidelines.

Confetti Cookies N' Cream
Blondies

blackberry bramble cheesecake blondies

makes 12 large squares or 24 smaller bars

I can't remember the last time I bought blackberries in a store, but I know they are not nearly as sweet and juicy as the wild ones my husband Don picks for me every summer, coming back with his arms and hands scratched from picking them in thick blackberry "bramble" patches. I freeze them in 9-ounce portions in vacuum sealed bags to use in this and other recipes all year round.

blackberry sauce
2 cups (9 ounces) fresh or frozen (unthawed) blackberries
½ cup (3.5 ounces) sugar
1 tablespoon cornstarch

blondie batter
Vegetable shortening for pan
1½ sticks (6 ounces) unsalted butter
6 ounces premium white baking chocolate
4 large eggs, at room temperature
2 cups (14 ounces) sugar
1 teaspoon salt
2 teaspoons pure vanilla extract
2½ cups (11.5 ounces) unbleached all-purpose flour
½ teaspoon baking powder

vanilla cheesecake batter
2 packages (8-ounces each) cream cheese, at room temperature
¼ teaspoon salt
$2/3$ cup (4.7 ounces) sugar
2 large egg yolks, at room temperature
2 teaspoons pure vanilla extract

1   To make the blackberry sauce, combine the blackberries, sugar, and cornstarch in a 1-quart saucier (or saucepan). Cover the pan tightly and cook over medium-low heat, stirring occasionally with a silicone spatula until the sugar dissolves, about 8-10 minutes. Increase the heat to high and bring to a boil, stirring constantly with the spatula until the mixture is quite thick, about 1 minute. Push the sauce through a medium-mesh strainer into a medium bowl, pressing on the berries with the spatula; discard the solids. Transfer the strained sauce to a 1-cup (Pyrex) measuring cup. Refrigerate the sauce while proceeding with the recipe.

2   Adjust an oven rack to the middle level of the oven and preheat to 350°F. Prepare a 9 by 13-inch baking pan with heavy-duty aluminum foil as shown on page ix. Lightly grease the foil in the pan.

3   To make the blondie batter, cut the butter sticks into ½-inch slices. In a small, heavy saucepan, melt the butter pieces over the lowest setting. While the butter is melting, chop the white chocolate very finely and add to the melted butter. Stir with a small whisk until combined and the white chocolate is melted and smooth. Remove the pan from the heat and set aside.

4   Using a large whisk, lightly beat the eggs in a large mixing bowl. Place the sugar and salt in a separate small mixing bowl, then whisk into the eggs just until incorporated. Briefly whisk the melted chocolate mixture, then gradually whisk into the egg mixture until just combined. Briefly whisk in the vanilla.

5   Place the flour and baking powder in the small mixing bowl; whisk together to combine. Sift through a medium strainer directly onto the batter; stir in with a silicone spatula until just combined. Scrape half (1 pound 8 ounces) of the blondie batter into the prepared pan. The best way to do this is by weight. Place the prepared pan on a scale, tare off (subtract) the weight of the pan, and scrape the correct weight of batter directly into the pan. Spread the batter evenly with a small offset spatula. Bake for 18 minutes, until a toothpick inserted in the center of the slab comes out clean and the top is nicely browned. Transfer the pan to a cooling rack.

6   Pour the cooled blackberry sauce into a 12-ounce squeeze bottle. Note: If you do not have a squeeze bottle, pour the blackberry sauce into a 2-cup Pyrex measuring cup. Pour three-quarters of the sauce over the bottom baked blondie layer, then use a spatula to drizzle the remaining sauce later over the unbaked cheesecake batter.

7   Squeeze about three-quarters of the blackberry sauce (leaving about an inch of the sauce in the bottom of the bottle) evenly in lines over the bottom baked blondie layer to within 1-inch of the pan sides; the sauce will not cover all of the baked blondie. Dollop the remaining blondie batter evenly over the top of the blackberry sauce; even out the batter with an offset spatula. Bake for 25 minutes, until a toothpick inserted near the center of the slab comes out clean and the top is nicely browned. Transfer the pan to a cooling rack. Maintain the oven temperature at 350°F. Prepare the vanilla cheesecake batter while the blondie slab is cooling at room temperature.

8   To make the vanilla cheesecake batter, cut the cream cheese into 1-inch slices and place in the small mixing bowl; add the salt. Using a hand mixer on high speed, beat until creamy. On medium speed, gradually add the sugar and beat an additional minute, scraping the bowl once to make sure the mixture is perfectly smooth. Add the egg yolks and vanilla, beat until just combined. Scrape down the sides of the bowl and beat again briefly. Dollop the cheesecake batter over the slightly cooled blondie layer and spread evenly with a small offset spatula.

9   Holding the bottle perpendicularly to the slab, squeeze the remaining blackberry sauce randomly in dots and "spurts" over the cheesecake batter. Return the pan to the oven and bake an additional 15 minutes, until the cheesecake layer is set when the pan is gently jiggled. Transfer the pan to a cooling rack and let cool at room temperature for 30 minutes; the cheesecake layer will continue to set up as it cools. Refrigerate the pan for 7 to 8 hours. See page xii for instructions on removing and cutting the slab, and for refrigerated storage (up to 1 week) and freezing guidelines.

Blackberry Bramble
Cheesecake Blondies

blanc et noir chocolate cheesecake blondies

makes 12 large squares or 24 smaller bars

Let's talk about blondies. Most people associate a "blondie" with a glorified version of a chocolate chip cookie, and I have versions like that (only better) included in both of my books. However, if I had my way, a true blondie would always be made with a white chocolate batter. Brownies must have chocolate in the batter, so why not blondies? This beautiful white chocolate blondie, with splotches of rich chocolate cheesecake piped inside, makes for a simply elegant dessert when plated with a few fresh raspberries.

blondie batter

Vegetable shortening for pan
1½ sticks (6 ounces) unsalted butter
6 ounces premium white baking chocolate
4 large eggs, at room temperature
2 cups (14 ounces) sugar
1 teaspoon salt
2 teaspoons pure vanilla extract
2½ cups (11.5 ounces) unbleached all-purpose flour
½ teaspoon baking powder

chocolate cheesecake batter

1 cup (6 ounces) 60% cacao bittersweet chocolate chips
6 ounces (three-quarters of an 8-ounce package) cream cheese, at room temperature
$1/8$ teaspoon salt
½ cup (3.5 ounces) sugar
$1/3$ cup and 1 tablespoon (3.3 ounces) sour cream, at room temperature
1 large egg, at room temperature

1 teaspoon pure chocolate extract
2 teaspoons Dutch-processed unsweetened cocoa powder

chocolate glaze

1 stick (4 ounces) unsalted butter
1 tablespoon and 1 teaspoon (1 ounce) light corn syrup
$1^1/3$ cups (8 ounces) 60% cacao bittersweet chocolate chips

garnish

2 ounces (half a bar/package) premium white baking chocolate

1   Fit a medium (14-inch) pastry bag with a ¼-inch round plain pastry tip (Ateco #803) using a large coupler, so that the metal pastry tip is on the outside of the bag and can be removed if necessary. Set aside to use later with the cheesecake batter.

2   Adjust an oven rack to the middle level of the oven and preheat to 350°F. Prepare a 9 by 13-inch baking pan with heavy-duty aluminum foil as shown on page ix. Lightly grease the foil in the pan.

3   To make the blondie batter, cut the butter sticks into ½-inch slices. In a small, heavy saucepan melt the butter pieces over the lowest setting. While the butter is melting, chop the white chocolate very finely and add to the melted butter. Stir with a small whisk until combined and the white chocolate is melted and smooth. Remove the pan from the heat and set aside.

4   Using a large whisk, lightly beat the eggs in a large mixing bowl. Place the sugar and salt in a separate small mixing bowl, then whisk into the eggs just until incorporated. Briefly whisk the melted chocolate mixture, then gradually whisk into the egg mixture until just combined. Briefly whisk in the vanilla. Note: Set aside the saucepan and small whisk (no need to wash them) to use later for the chocolate glaze.

5   Place the flour and baking powder in the small mixing bowl; whisk together to combine. Sift through a medium strainer directly onto the batter; stir in with a silicone spatula until just combined. Scrape the batter into the prepared pan and spread evenly with a small offset spatula. Set aside.

6   To make the chocolate cheesecake batter, place the chocolate chips in a 2-cup Pyrex measuring cup. Microwave the chips on high power for 90 seconds, stir with a small silicone spatula, then microwave an additional 15 seconds. Stir until the chocolate is melted and smooth. Set aside to cool at room temperature.

7   Cut the cream cheese into 1-inch slices and place in the now empty small mixing bowl; add the salt. Using a hand mixer on high speed, beat until smooth

Blanc Et Noir
Chocolate Cheesecake Blondies

and creamy. On medium speed, add the sugar and beat an additional minute, scraping the bowl with a silicone spatula once to make sure the mixture is perfectly smooth. Add the sour cream, egg, and chocolate extract; beat until just combined. Slowly beat in the melted chocolate until just combined. Sift the cocoa powder through a medium strainer directly onto the cheesecake batter; stir in with the spatula to combine. Use a silicone spatula to dollop the chocolate cheesecake batter into the prepared pastry bag. Note: Set aside the Pyrex measuring cup (no need to wash it) to use later for the chocolate glaze.

8   Using the pastry bag, push the pastry tip down into the blondie batter to the bottom of the pan. Pipe random dots of chocolate cheesecake batter into the blondie batter. If the cheesecake dots look "hollow" fill them in with additional cheesecake batter. Use the tip of a finger to smooth out the top of each cheesecake mound. The blondie batter will slightly rise in each area as you pipe in the cheesecake batter, and the top of the batter will not be flat. It will even out during baking.

9   Bake for 30 minutes, until a toothpick inserted in the center of the slab comes out clean and the top is nicely browned. Transfer the pan to a cooling rack.

10 To make the chocolate glaze, slice the butter into ¼-inch slices. Place the butter slices and corn syrup in the reserved small saucepan and melt over the lowest setting. Meanwhile, place the chocolate chips in the reserved measuring cup. Microwave the chips on high power for 90 seconds, whisk with the reserved small whisk, then microwave an additional 15 seconds: whisk again. Pour the melted butter mixture into the melted chocolate and whisk gently until combined and completely smooth. Pour the glaze over the blondie slab and spread evenly with a small offset spatula. Place the pan in the refrigerator for 20 minutes to cool down the glaze.

11 To make the garnish, hold the half-bar of white chocolate in your hand. Using a vegetable peeler, shave off curls of white chocolate around the edges of the bar directly onto the chocolate glaze. Continuously turn the half-bar as you shave off curls: the warm edges where you were holding the white chocolate will help create nicer curls. Continue until the half-bar is gone and the chocolate glaze is covered in white chocolate curls. Refrigerate the pan for 7 to 8 hours, or overnight. See page xii for instructions on removing and cutting the slab, and for refrigerated storage (up to 2 weeks) and freezing guidelines.

note

Because the chocolate cheesecake has melted chocolate in it, it has to be made at the last minute or the chocolate will start to cool and become too thick to pipe. For this recipe, I feel it is a MUST that the pastry bag be fitted with a large pastry bag coupler to hold the pastry tip. If during the piping process the chocolate cheesecake becomes too thick to pipe, you can unscrew the top of the coupler, remove the metal pastry tip, and place the pastry bag with the cheesecake batter in the microwave for 15 to 20 seconds to warm/thin out the batter. If the metal pastry tip is placed inside the bag not using a coupler, you cannot put the bag in the microwave because the metal tip cannot go in the microwave.

vanilla bean cheesecake chocolate chip blondies

makes 12 large squares or 24 smaller bars

People have been baking brownies with a layer of cheesecake for years, and my current version of that is my Chic Chevron Cheesecake Brownie. I thought it was time for a good blondie to have the same type of cheesecake pairing. This blondie tastes like a fabulous chocolate chip cookie topped with the most delicious vanilla bean cheesecake ever!

---

blondie batter
Vegetable shortening for pan
2 sticks (8 ounces) unsalted butter
2 large eggs, at room temperature
2 teaspoons pure vanilla bean paste
1¾ packed cups (14 ounces) light brown sugar
1 teaspoon salt
1¹⁄₈ teaspoons baking powder
2¹⁄₃ cups (10.5 ounces) unbleached all-purpose flour
1 cup (6 ounces) 63% extra dark chocolate chips

vanilla bean cheesecake batter
3 (8-ounce) packages cream cheese, at room temperature
½ teaspoon salt
1 cup (7 ounces) sugar
1 large egg, at room temperature
1 large egg white, at room temperature
1 tablespoon pure vanilla bean paste

garnish
2 to 3 tablespoons 63% extra dark chocolate chips

1 Adjust an oven rack to the middle level of the oven and preheat to 350°F.

2 To make the blondie batter, cut the butter sticks into ½-inch slices. Place the butter slices in a heavy 1-quart saucepan. Cook over the lowest setting until the butter melts, stirring frequently with a silicone spatula. Remove the pan from the heat and let the butter cool to lukewarm while proceeding with the recipe.

3 Prepare a 9 by 13-inch baking pan with heavy-duty aluminum foil as shown on page ix. Lightly grease the foil in the pan.

4 Place the eggs and vanilla bean paste in the bowl of a stand mixer fitted with the paddle attachment. Place the brown sugar, salt, and baking powder in a small mixing bowl, then add to the egg mixture. On medium speed, beat the mixture for 2 to 3 minutes, just until light in color and slightly thickened.

5   Reduce the mixer speed to the lowest speed and very slowly drizzle in the melted butter.

6   On the lowest speed, very gradually add the flour and beat until just combined. Remove the bowl and paddle from the mixer stand; add any batter from the paddle to the bowl. Fold the batter with a spatula to make sure all of the ingredients are incorporated. Dollop ½ cup (4.5 ounces) of the batter into a 1-cup Pyrex measuring cup. The best way to do this is by weight. Place the cup on a scale, tare off (subtract) the weight of the cup, then dollop the correct amount of batter directly into the cup. Set aside.

7   Pour the chocolate chips over the batter remaining in the mixing bowl and fold in with a silicone spatula. Dollop the batter into the prepared pan and spread evenly with a small offset spatula. Bake at 350°F for 24 minutes, until a toothpick inserted in the center of the slab comes out clean and the top is nicely browned. Transfer the pan to a cooling rack. Maintain the oven temperature at 350°F. Prepare the vanilla bean cheesecake batter while the blondie slab is cooling at room temperature.

8   Place a small (10-inch) pastry bag fitted with a ½-inch round plain pastry tip (Ateco #806) inside of a glass, with the edges of the pastry bag hanging over the sides of the glass. Set aside.

9   To make the vanilla bean cheesecake batter, cut the cream cheese into 1-inch slices and place in the bowl of a stand mixer fitted with the paddle attachment: add the salt. Beat together on medium speed for 1 minute. On medium speed, gradually add the sugar and beat an additional 2 minutes, scraping the bowl once to make sure the mixture is perfectly smooth. Add the egg, egg white, and vanilla bean paste: beat on medium speed until just combined. Dollop the cheesecake batter over the blondie layer and spread evenly with a small offset spatula.

10 Gently warm the reserved blondie batter in a microwave oven set on 50% power until just warm, about 15 to 20 seconds. Transfer the warmed batter to the pastry bag. Pipe random "spots" of the reserved blondie batter over the cheesecake batter. Don't be concerned if the blondie batter sticks up above the cheesecake layer; it will level out as it bakes. Place the chocolate chips randomly around the blondie batter spots. Bake an additional 28 minutes, until the cheesecake layer moves as a mass when the pan is gently jiggled, the blondie spots are set and lightly browned, and tiny cracks are around the edges of the cheesecake. Transfer the pan to a cooling rack and let cool at room temperature for 30 minutes; the cheesecake layer will continue to set up as it cools. Refrigerate the pan for 7 to 8 hours, or overnight. See page xii for instructions on removing and cutting the slab, and for refrigerated storage (up to 2 weeks) and freezing guidelines.

Vanilla Bean Cheesecake
Chocolate Chip Blondies

metric
conversions
and equivalents

<table>
<tr><td colspan="2">metric conversion formulas</td><td colspan="2">approixmate metric equivalents</td></tr>
<tr><td>to convert</td><td>multiply</td><td colspan="2">volume</td></tr>
<tr><td>Ounces to grams</td><td>Ounces by 28.35</td><td>¼ teaspoon</td><td>1 milliliter</td></tr>
<tr><td>Pounds to kilograms</td><td>Pounds by 0.454</td><td>½ teaspoon</td><td>2.5 milliliters</td></tr>
<tr><td>Teaspoons to milliliters</td><td>Teaspoons by 4.93</td><td>¾ teaspoon</td><td>4 milliliters</td></tr>
<tr><td>Tablespoons to milliliters</td><td>Tablespoons by 14.79</td><td>1 teaspoon</td><td>5 milliliters</td></tr>
<tr><td>Fluid ounces to milliliters</td><td>Fluid ounces by 29.57</td><td>1¼ teaspoons</td><td>6 milliliters</td></tr>
<tr><td>Cups to milliliters</td><td>Cups by 236.59</td><td>1½ teaspoons</td><td>7.5 milliliters</td></tr>
<tr><td>Cups to liters</td><td>Cups by 0.236</td><td>1¾ teaspoons</td><td>8.5 milliliters</td></tr>
<tr><td>Pints to liters</td><td>Pints by 0.473</td><td>2 teaspoons</td><td>10 milliliters</td></tr>
<tr><td>Quarts to liters</td><td>Quarts by 0.946</td><td>1 tablespoon (0.5 fluid ounce)</td><td>15 milliliters</td></tr>
<tr><td>Gallons to liters</td><td>Gallons by 3.785</td><td>2 tablespoons (1 fluid ounce)</td><td>30 milliliters</td></tr>
<tr><td>Inches to centimeters</td><td>Inches by 2.54</td><td>¼ cup</td><td>60 milliliters</td></tr>
<tr><td></td><td></td><td>⅓ cup</td><td>80 milliliters</td></tr>
<tr><td></td><td></td><td>½ cup (4 fluid ounces)</td><td>120 milliliters</td></tr>
<tr><td></td><td></td><td>⅔ cup</td><td>160 milliliters</td></tr>
<tr><td></td><td></td><td>¾ cup</td><td>180 milliliters</td></tr>
<tr><td></td><td></td><td>1 cup (8 fluid ounces)</td><td>240 milliliters</td></tr>
<tr><td></td><td></td><td>1¼ cups</td><td>300 milliliters</td></tr>
<tr><td></td><td></td><td>1½ cups (12 fluid ounces)</td><td>360 milliliters</td></tr>
<tr><td></td><td></td><td>1⅔ cups</td><td>400 milliliters</td></tr>
<tr><td></td><td></td><td>2 cups (1 pint)</td><td>460 milliliters</td></tr>
<tr><td></td><td></td><td>3 cups</td><td>700 milliliters</td></tr>
<tr><td></td><td></td><td>4 cups (1 quart)</td><td>0.95 liter</td></tr>
<tr><td></td><td></td><td>1 quart plus ¼ cup</td><td>1 liter</td></tr>
<tr><td></td><td></td><td>4 quarts (1 gallon)</td><td>3.8 liters</td></tr>
</table>

weight

0.25 ounce	7 grams
0.5 ounce	14 grams
0.75 ounce	21 grams
1 ounce	28 grams
1.25 ounces	35 grams
1.5 ounces	42.5 grams
1.666 ounces	45 grams
2 ounces	57 grams
3 ounces	85 grams
4 ounces (¼ pound)	113 grams
5 ounces	142 grams
6 ounces	170 grams
7 ounces	198 grams
8 ounces (½ pound)	227 grams
16 ounces (1 pound)	454 grams
35.25 ounces (2.2 pounds)	1 kilogram

length

⅛ inch	3 millimeters
¼ inch	6 millimeters
½ inch	1.25 centimeters
1 inch	2.5 centimeters
2 inches	5 centimeters
2½ inches	6 centimeters
4 inches	10 centimeters
5 inches	13 centimeters
6 inches	15.25 centimeters
12 inches (1 foot)	30 centimeters

oven temperatures

To convert Fahrenheit to Celsius, subtract 32 from Fahrenheit, multiply the result by 5, then divide by 9.

description	fahrenheit	celsius	british gas mark
Very cool	200°	95°	0
Very cool	225°	110°	¼
Very cool	250°	120°	½
Cool	275°	135°	1
Cool	300°	150°	2
Warm	325°	165°	3
Moderate	350°	175°	4
Moderately hot	375°	190°	5
Fairly hot	400°	200°	6
Hot	425°	220°	7
Very hot	450°	230°	8
Very hot	475°	245°	9

common ingredients and their approixmate equivalents

1 cup all-purpose flour = 140 grams
1 stick butter (4 ounces • ½ cup • 8 tablespoons) = 110g
1 cup butter (8 ounces • 2 sticks • 16 tablespoons) = 220g
1 cup brown sugar, firmly packed = 225 grams
1 cup granulated sugar = 200 grams

index